ART for the EXCEPTIONAL

ART for the EXCEPTIONAL

Chester J. Alkema

Pruett Publishing Company

Boulder, Colorado

10403

I dedicate this book to exceptional children everywhere, whose creative talents are waiting to be discovered, explored and expressed; and to their teachers, whose patience, love and understanding provide the proper atmosphere for self-expression in art which contributes immeasurably to the mental, social-emotional and motor development of exceptional children.

Chester J. Alkema

Contents

Preface

Figure 1. The author encourages Michigan State University students to work with a variety of art materials so that they may better identify with the creative needs of their exceptional pupils.

Photo, courtesy of Information Services, Michigan State University.

When working on the Master of Fine Arts degree at Michigan State University, Mr. Alkema began research on the topic, "Art for Teachers of the Exceptional." His prepared bibliography, "Art for Teachers of the Exceptional, A Selected Bibliography by Chester Jay Alkema," is the first and only existing bibliography on this subject.

Subsequently, the art department of MSU invited Mr. Alkema to introduce and teach a new course in art for teachers of the exceptional. Since its inception, the course has been taught repeatedly at MSU by Mr. Alkema in East Lansing and Grand Rapids, and more recently at Grand Valley State College, Allendale, Michigan.

The author sets forth a few of the many ideas presented and discussed in his classes. The ideas have evolved from research and experience in working with children, and result from the needs and questions posed by the dedicated teachers and prospective teachers who have been his students at Michigan State University and Grand Valley State College.

Introduction

Creative art experiences offer a multitude of values relative to the mental, social-emotional and motor development of children. When a child is given the freedom to express his own ideas as they relate to his own thoughts and feelings, he learns to think independently. Mental development is fostered. He is encouraged to be an individual, to be original in terms of self-expression. New ideas are constantly discovered. His mind continually searches for new solutions to old problems. Through experimentation, the student learns to correct his "mistakes" as mental awareness increases. The creative process helps the child to organize his ideas in an ever-growing system of orderliness. He learns to use the elements of art, lines, shapes, colors, textures, movements, etc., so that they become orderly, expressive and beautiful. Artistic expression encourages the child to observe his environment more closely and to recall more vividly what he has seen. Art contributes greatly to the mental development of the young artist.

The social-emotional development of the child is also fostered by creative art expressions. Art can be therapeutic when the artist chooses his own experiences, repeats them and varies them at will. In choosing these experiences, the artist must face, relive and resolve his inner conflicts and fears. He can tell of his feelings of hate as well as love and joy. Through art, he can effectively speak about himself. Any student of psychology realizes how important the act of self-expression can be in the continuing social and emotional development of the individual.

Art also plays a role in the motor development of the child. Better coordination and muscular control develop through the manipulation of a variety of art materials. Hand and eye coordination improves, for example, when the brush and paint are used to express oneself.

When art is viewed in terms of the exceptional child, these values as well as others take on a new meaning, an added significance. The diverse needs of exceptional children cause us to re-evaluate our objectives, to search for new and better motivational procedures and teaching methods, to discover more appropriate art materials and techniques for using them. The great challenge of teaching the exceptional child necessitates a constant search for new methods by which the important developmental values of art may be realized. This is accomplished by research, study, experience, patience and understanding, common sense, a love of mankind and that wonderful attribute, empathy.

Let us consider the exceptional child and note how some of his problems affect himself and therefore the teacher of art.

The Physically Handicapped Child

We live in a society that idolizes the Elizabeth Taylors and Rock Hudsons of our day. The millions of dollars spent annually on cosmetics and the latest fashions in clothing are evidence of the emphasis we place on bodily perfection and beauty. It is not easy for the physically handicapped to adjust to a society which holds these ideals. The individual who is physically disabled early in life must constantly meet the challenge of self-acceptance. While one person is able to meet this challenge readily, another may require outside help. Others never do learn to accept their handicaps. The person who is disabled in later life must at times fight a battle far more severe than the person who has spent a lifetime learning that life still has much to offer. The secondary handicap (the feelings he has about himself) may cause the individual far more suffering than the primary handicap (the actual physical disability).

We all have a mental image of ourselves. By means of this mental image we may think we have a fairly accurate conception of the way we appear to others. Often, however, there is or can be a great discrepancy between the way we see ourselves and the way others see us. The crippled child can easily develop an exaggerated mental image of the self. He cannot accept his defect, for he is sure others do not. Self-pity and self-doubts blur his vision. Professional help may be needed to improve the individual's self-image. One of our large mental institutions is helping patients gain back their self-respect with some measure of success. Motion pictures are taken of the patient, and closed-circuit television is also used. By viewing the self on the screen at frequent intervals, the patient gains a truer picture of the way he looks in the eyes of other people. The patient's feelings which relate to the handicap come into a healthier perspective through self-observation.

Art experiences can also play a major role in bringing about this change of inner feelings. Under normal conditions the young child has few qualms about describing his mental image of himself in his art work. Most of his work includes the self. He is very egotistical. The world centers about himself. But this is true only under normal conditions, when the child accepts himself. Not only may the crippled child lack this self-acceptance, but he may consequently refuse to express the self in his art work. Or, if the self does appear in the art product, it may reveal a highly repetitious or stereotyped version of his body. It now becomes the task of the art teacher to strongly motivate the child in art so that he faces the self in his art product, so that he presents himself in a more flexible manner. The proper motivation can be effective only when the teacher seriously considers the interests and experiences of the child. These interests and experiences are important in drawing the child out of his protective shell. Through creative art experiences the handicapped child may profit greatly, to the extent that actual changes occur in his personality.

Art experiences can also be a way of performing mentally a desired activity which it is impossible to do physically. The severely crippled often wish they could swim or dance. Instead of just thinking of the impossible, the patient might be encouraged to paint himself performing

3

these coveted activities.   He not only faces his limitations when executing the art product, but also drains the pent-up emotions associated with his limited physical capacities.

We have seen how art experiences can contribute in healing the secondary handicap, i.e., the feelings concerning the physical handicap.   Art involvement can also be instrumental in improving the primary handicap.   For example, the cerebral palsied or the arthritic patient can improve the muscular coordination of the hands and fingers by kneading and squeezing clay.   Better hand and eye coordination can be attained when the cerebral palsied are strongly motivated to express their ideas using a brush and controllable paint.

Some forms of therapy are necessary in treating the physical handicap of the patient but at the same time cause a digressive pattern in the patient's social behavior.   The polio patient, for example, may need daily baths to restore or improve muscular coordination in his legs.   But each time the patient takes his bath, he is reminded of his physical disability.   The defective members of his body gain an abnormal prominence in his mind.   There are times when creative art activities may provide a most effective kind of therapy.   For example, the patient might use his weakened leg to operate the pedal of a loom.   While working, his mind is not on the exercising leg but on the object he is creating on the loom.   All undesirable attitudes will give way to the thoughts and emotional feelings associated with the creative activity.

The product of the physically handicapped will often appear immature, his progress less discernible than that of the normal child.   It is most important for the teacher to give strong encouragement and recognition when deserved.   Progress is often slow, and the patient easily becomes discouraged.

Figure 2.   When a patient is unable to use his fingers, a long brush taped to the patient's arm allows him to use arm movements in executing his painting.

SPECIAL TECHNIQUES

Whenever possible, the defective member of the body should be used in manipulating art materials so that muscular strength and control may be achieved.   There are times, however, when the patient and teacher must make certain improvisations.   If the hands cannot be used, new ways of expressing the self must be found.   A long brush may be taped to the patient's arm, thus allowing him to use arm movements in executing his painting (Figure 2).   If both arms and hands are functionless, it may become necessary for the patient to use his feet and toes. Flat pans of paint may be set upon the floor. Seated in a chair, the patient can apply the paint with the toes and feet to a large sheet of paper taped to the wall, a few inches above the floor. Valuable suggestions related to this approach may be found in the article, "Foot Painting," *Design*, Spring 1970, pp. 22-24.

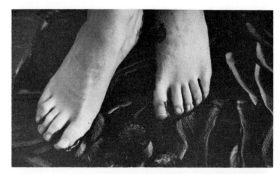

Figure 3 (below). If both arms and hands are functionless, it may become necessary for the patient to use his feet and toes.

Figure 4 (right, above). Commercial finger paint, applied to a commercial glazed finger paint paper or shiny shelf paper, enables the patient to create a variety of effects with his feet.

Figure 5 (right, center). The toe may be used to create lines which are straight, curved or zig-zagged.

Figure 6 (right, below). The heel of the foot may be applied to create circles. Different effects are achieved by dabbing and twisting the heel on the surface of the paper.

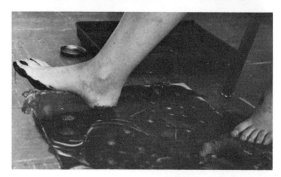

Figures 7 through 10.   Completed foot paintings executed with the toes and heel.

Some paralytics, unable to use either hands or feet, become quite competent in painting with a brush held by the teeth. Paper or canvas should be placed in a vertical position at a brush's length from the patient. The paints must also be placed at a brush's length from the patient's mouth.

A synthetic or natural sponge has proved to be of great value to certain patients. A string or ribbon inserted through the center of the sponge can be used to tie it to the arm, hand or foot. The sponge is superior to the brush in that it will hold more paint. It is a versatile painting instrument: the corner of the sponge can be used to make thin lines, and the flat side of the sponge produces broad, flat, sweeping areas of color. By dabbling the sponge on paper, a variety of textures can be easily created. The sponge allows the patient to work more quickly; this is important, as the patient can easily become discouraged when using the less controllable members of the body in art expression.

Whatever tool is used, it is important that the paint be mixed at least to the consistency of cream, if not thicker. Thin, watery paints are hard to manage and control, thus producing disappointing results. Powdered tempera paint is a far better choice. By varying the water content, the teacher can easily mix the paint to proper proportions. The older patient, particularly one who must use the brush held by the teeth, will enjoy working with oil paints as they are highly controllable.

At present, there is a national club consisting of some forty paralytic artists. Members exchange ideas and tell of their artistic endeavors. Since all members have a common problem, a common bond, the communications between members are rewarding and inspirational to all concerned. It is gratifying to know that the late Dwight D. Eisenhower was the proud owner of a painting created by a member of this club. The painting was executed by means of a brush held in the artist's teeth.

Figure 11. Glen Fowler, a member of the Association of Handicapped Artists, Inc., paints by mouth. Mr. Fowler is the recipient of many First Prize awards and is ranked among the most talented artists in his native Massachusetts. He was a prize winner of the 1960 Polio Foundation "Help the Handicapped" poster contest.
Photo, courtesy of the Association of Handicapped Artists, Inc.

The Emotionally Disturbed Child

In the dictionary we find the word "sublimate" defined in this way: "To direct the energy of an impulse from its primitive aim to one that is culturally or ethically higher." The word sublimation, then, is the key word in describing the value of art for the emotionally disturbed. The seemingly unmanageable classroom bully can sublimate his frustrations and aggressive behavior by pounding, kneading and shaping clay into forms dictated by his imagination. The child taught too early or severely in his toilet training or in personal neatness is able to release his anxieties by "messing" with paper maché, finger paints, clay and similar media. The young neurotic may likewise release his emotions through such an activity as finger painting. The schizophrenic patient eases his tensions by working with art materials. He appears less strained after his creative experience. The *act* of being creative is of great value to the emotionally disturbed.

Can art also be of value to the teacher in *diagnosing* causes for the child's behavior? Let me give a warning with this story.

The teacher, observing Johnny's art work, noticed that her young student was limiting himself to the color purple in nearly all of his drawings. She had heard that the exclusive use of purple indicated a rather serious emotional disturbance. Consequently, the child was sent to a clinic for a series of psychological tests. The results seemed to indicate little or no sign of any serious emotional difficulty. Finally Johnny was asked why he so often chose the color purple to portray his ideas. His answer: "It's the only color I have left in my crayon box."

The point is that most art teachers are not equipped or trained to judge behavior traits by the product of the child. In so doing, the teacher is likely to do more harm to the child than good. Choice of colors or repeated symbols should not be analyzed by the untrained. Personality diagnosis through the use of an art product must be done by a very special kind of person: he must not only be a competent teacher of art, but he must also be a trained psychologist. Those interested in art as a means of diagnosing the behavior traits of the neurotic can consult the excellent article by J. A. Arlow and A. L. Kadis, entitled "Finger Painting in the Psychotherapy of Children," which appeared in the *American Journal of Orthopsychiatry*, 1946, pp. 16, 134 and 146. The diagnostic values of art for the schizophrenic are discussed in the book by Margaret Naumberg, *Schizophrenic Art: Its Meaning in Psychotherapy*, Gruen and Stratton, N. Y., 1950. Viktor Lowenfeld's *Creative and Mental Growth*, Macmillan, N. Y., 1957, pp. 488-494, will also be of value in this area of study.

SPECIAL TECHNIQUES

Finger painting has commonly been recognized as an effective medium of expression for the emotionally disturbed. The child, afraid to express himself, soon loses his inhibitions in the joy of seeing the fascinating, rhythmic, free, contrasting lines appear on the white glossy paper. Finger painting allows the artist to use his large muscles. The playing of rhythmic music during the painting sessions contributes to an even greater freedom in self-expression.

Some emotionally disturbed patients have a tendency to put almost anything into their mouths. If such is the case, the teacher may substitute chocolate syrup for the regular paint. Chocolate syrup is of a proper consistency for finger painting on shiny paper, and offers a pleasing contrast to the white background (Figure 12).

Figure 12.   Chocolate syrup makes an excellent finger painting medium for the emotionally disturbed patient, who has a tendency to put almost anything in his mouth.

The Juvenile Delinquent

In considering the juvenile delinquent and art, we again find that the sublimation of emotional tensions is the secret of the successful use of art. The delinquent often holds deep resentment toward imaginary or real associates. He feels that he has been dealt with unjustly and that he must retaliate. His actions show little consideration for the welfare of others. Guidance counselors often find it difficult to communicate with the delinquent. It is hard to get at the root of his difficulties. What incidents in his life have contributed to his present behavioral pattern? Why the feelings of frustration and hatred? Sometimes the delinquent himself is not aware of the answers, and often he will refuse to discuss his innermost problems. Creative art experiences provide a most effective avenue of expression: the juvenile delinquent willingly "tells all" as the art product is executed, often without being consciously aware that he is doing so.

GROUP ACTIVITIES

Group activities can contribute greatly to the social-emotional growth of the juvenile delinquent. The joint-construction of a mural, a diorama or a puppet show, for example, necessitates a cooperative spirit among workers if the end product is to be achieved. In planning an activity each participant learns to evaluate and respect the opinions and ideas of others. Each learns that without the help of others the final product could not have come into existence. Associates are viewed as produc-

tive members of a better society. Each member comes to recognize his own worthiness. He consciously compares his endeavors with the work of others and realizes that he, too, has something to contribute to the final product. His contributions, when effectively performed, often win the approval and respect of his fellow workers. To paraphrase Webster, primitive impulses are redirected so that aims become culturally and ethically higher.

The Deaf Child

The problems of the deaf child contribute some of the greatest challenges to the teacher of art. Getting to the heart of these problems, we must conclude that the difficulty is associated with the child's lack of self-involvement in expressing himself. In his education, many of the deaf child's activities cause him to be dependent upon his teacher: he imitates her in learning to read lips, he follows her example in learning to communicate by means of the sign language, he repetitiously tries to parrot her methods of producing recognizable oral sounds, and he is dependent upon her in learning to associate words with objects. This reliance upon the teacher is carried over in the child's art performances. Often he will prefer to watch other members of the class carry out their projects (Figure 13). He may be perfectly content to have the teacher draw or paint for him. And this practice is devastating, since he is encouraged to become even more dependent upon his teacher. Another contributing factor to this lack of self-involvement stems from the lack of oral communication between other class members and the teacher. The young child who has not yet mastered the techniques of communicating his thoughts is greatly restricted in discussing his artistic expressions with others. The hearing child can magnify both the message of his art work and the pleasures associated with the activity by talking with the teacher and his friends, but the deaf are denied this. Greater self-involvement is possible only when the most effective methods of motivation are employed.

Art can be of tremendous value in contributing to the growth of the deaf. It allows the child to express feelings about himself and others, and it brings him into a closer relationship with his environment. Since verbal communication is slow in developing, this avenue of expression is greatly needed. Art can help the child to become independent in his thinking, to make his own decisions and discoveries, to experiment with new ideas. For the child who must rely on others for much of his learning, these values cannot be overemphasized. Art can be effective in the development of lip reading and object-word associations. The student will watch the teacher's lips as she discusses his product. "I like your painting, Jane. This is you, Jane. This is your doll." As the teacher points to various objects in the painting, the student learns to identify familiar contents verbally during one of the most pleasurable activities of the school day.

SPECIAL TECHNIQUES

Motivating the young deaf person offers a seemingly insurmountable challenge to the teacher of art. How can one motivate a young child when he cannot understand the spoken word? Pictures may offer one solution to the problem of stimulating interest in a topic suitable for expression. Teachers of the deaf usually have files filled with pictures of various objects and activities. Such pictures are needed in helping the deaf learn to associate objects with the written word. A few pictures depicting children at play in the snow will soon communicate a broad, general topic such as "Games we like to play in the wintertime." Children themselves may suggest a topic by means of bodily activity.

A child who lies on a table and moves both arms back and forth is showing the class that he is going to paint a picture entitled, "I am steering my sled down the hill." Another child pushing an imaginary object may be saying, "Let's paint a picture of us building a snowman." By going through the motions of a favored activity, the child can better identify with his topic. The actual performance of the action helps the child to portray the self more effectively. The movements and motions help to stir the imagination. Ideas begin to grow. To get the activity started, the teacher may want to pantomime various activities that she associates with the topic.

To motivate the child effectively, the teacher must be aware of his interests and experiences. And since the young child cannot tell of these experiences, the teacher must discover them in other ways. She will closely observe him in play during his free time. A conference with the parents will reveal much more. If the child draws or paints during his spare time, what does he say in his art work? The art product may be a starting point for encouraging the child to expand his interests and to express the expanded knowledge associated with his original idea. All art work of the child should be examined closely for clues relating to his favorite activities and experiences.

The deaf child's handicap does not necessarily warrant the choosing of special art materials. A *variety* of art materials should be provided so that the student may have a choice in selecting the most effective and pleasurable means of expression.

Figure 13. The young deaf child, reliant upon his teacher for so many aspects of his training, is often content to just watch others work. Lack of verbal communication also contributes to this absence of self-involvement in creative art experiences.

The Gifted Child

Figure 14. The painting "Autumn Trees" by eight-year-old Mark reveals many attributes of the young gifted artist.

Photo, courtesy of Information Services, Michigan State University.

others. The gifted use their fluent imaginations to produce work that is sensitive, original and of a high esthetic standard. They have a strong feeling for life. Ideas are expressed with great intensity. The gifted are easily motivated. For them it is easy to expand and build upon a single suggested idea. They quickly discover not only the limitations but also the possibilities of working with their art materials when executing their ideas.

The painting "Autumn Trees" by eight-year-old Mark (Figure 14) reveals these attributes. Mark's paints have been handled in a luminous, soft and subtle manner. The dynamics of the lights and darks are most exciting to the eye. Textures, hues and diverse values have been carefully repeated so as to create a pleasing balance. The placement of objects reveals a carefully organized, balanced composition. There is a perfect relationship of parts. One does not wish to make changes in the painting: it seems just right. Mark's alert, observing eyes allow him to see how trees really grow, how they branch out from the trunk into ever smaller branches. The placement of objects and the gradation of tones from dark to light all help to suggest space effectively. Mark is able to identify with his subject and has the ability to execute it well.

It is not uncommon to encounter certain misconceptions regarding the attributes of the young gifted artist. Recently I was shown a number of portraits sketched in pencil by a young junior high student. Each photographic likeness of the human face revealed a repetitious similarity to others in the group. The position and shape of the heads, the execution of the facial features showed that the student could produce a stereotyped, slick portrait with great ease. The teacher considered this child to be gifted in art. Another teacher brought pen and ink sketches by her student to class along with the originals from which they had been copied. To her, the ability to copy perfectly the style and technique of another artist proved the student to be a gifted artist.

A person who is truly gifted in art is not content to be repetitious in expressing his ideas. He is by no means satisfied to copy the ideas of

Other attributes of Mark's which typify the gifted are his high I.Q., his interest in areas other than art and his impressive ability to achieve in many activities. For Mark it is an easy matter to solve the diverse problems relating to his studies.

From this description of the gifted, one might think that they can be easily taught, that their problems are few.   This is not necessarily true. While it is relatively easy to motivate the gifted in art, guidance on the part of the teacher is far more difficult.   Because solutions to problems usually come quickly to the gifted, an especially difficult problem may result in rapid discouragement.   The right suggestions and words of encouragement by the teacher are necessary to revitalize the child's thinking and to activate a new interest in concluding a project.   The teacher must challenge the students every step of the way, as they easily become bored.   Usually the gifted are mercilessly hard on themselves. Inwardly, they want the teacher to be equally hard on them.   They want to be directed continually to seeing new problems.

In the average classroom, the gifted will often prefer to work alone. They cannot fully understand or identify with their associates' lower levels of achievement.   For the gifted child's own good, it is advantageous to assign him to a group project.   He must learn that he is not the only person with abilities.   The contributions of others may help him to realize that certain aspects of a job can be carried out equally well by others.   Undue conceit can be one of the pitfalls of the gifted.

Some gifted children are best challenged by outside opportunity classes. Large city school systems often provide a single class for the gifted in art.   This kind of competition will often place the gifted child in a better position to evaluate his own talents realistically.   Evening university classes and museum classes may also provide the proper challenge.

Teachers must use discretion when recognizing the artistic talents of the gifted.   Their achievements should not be singled out from the endeavors of their peers, as this can be disadvantageous to both the gifted child and his classmates.   One must be careful not to place too many pressures upon the capable shoulders of the gifted child.

The Mentally Retarded Child

A mentally retarded individual does not have the mental capacity or the level of achievement reached by others of the same chronological age. Michael, aged six, mentally retarded and a victim of cerebral palsy, was motivated to draw a picture relating to the subject of apples (Figure 15). A class trip to an apple orchard revealed to Michael how apples grew on trees, how they were picked and stored. Although Michael was interested in his topic, he was found lacking in the ability to express his ideas. The timid, non-rhythmic, cramped, unrelated lines point out his lack of coordination and also his delayed stage of artistic development. Michael performs like a child a few years younger, one who is

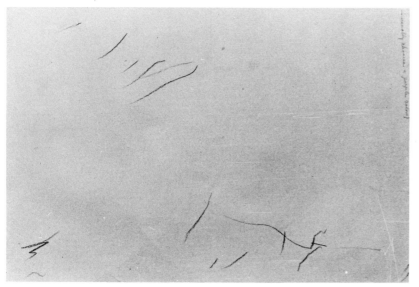

Figure 15. Michael, aged six, mentally retarded and a victim of cerebral palsy, is unable to use recognizable symbols in expressing his ideas. The timid, cramped lines are indicative of the child's lack of coordination.

Figure 16. A few months later, Michael is able to make curved lines, rhythmically flowing in a circular movement, indicating an improvement in muscular control. However, recognizable symbols do not yet appear.

still in the scribbling stage.   A few months after making this drawing, Michael was motivated to react to the topic, "Riding to School."   The teacher asked, "How do you come to school in the morning?   By car?   Bus?   What does the bus look like?   What are its colors?   Does it have windows and doors?"   The second example of Michael's work (Figure 16) reveals a marked improvement in muscular control.   The tight, disconnected lines are replaced by curved lines, rhythmically flowing in a circular movement.   Recognizable symbols, however, do not

Figure 17 (above).   Compare Michael's art work with that of Barth. Having the same chronological age, but a normal I. Q., Barth is easily able to produce symbols which express his ideas.

Figure 18 (right).   The painting "Autumn Trees" by John, age eight and mentally retarded, reveals marked differences in artistic achievement when compared with the gifted child's rendition of the same subject (Figure 14).

yet appear. Compare Michael's second drawing with Barth's (Figure 17.) Barth, also six years old but having a normal I.Q., is able to use symbols in expressing his idea. We clearly see a bus with Barth in the doorway, windows revealing faces looking out, Barth's home and a bright sun shedding its rays of light. With a little more time to grow, Michael too may reach an advanced stage of artistic development.

John, aged eight and also mentally retarded, has painted the picture, "Autumn Trees" (Figure 18). He is able to produce symbols of his subject, trees. A comparison of this painting with the gifted child's rendition of the same subject (Figure 14) reveals striking differences in artistic achievement. John's painting lacks balance, in that the top half of the composition is completely unthought of. Both trees are repetitions of each other and therefore lack variety. Other paintings of John's reveal this same monotonous, stereotyped, restricted and unvaried symbol for the tree. Little interest in color is evident. Although more than one color was at John's disposal, he chose black, which happened to be conveniently near at hand. We see then a lack of variety in the use of color, light and dark tones, tints, shading and texture. Depth and space have not been realized.

If John is to improve in his ability to express himself, the teacher may have to motivate and guide him more effectively so that his mental perception of the subject will be more conclusive and vital. Or it may be advisable to stimulate John into expressing a completely new idea, one that is more in keeping with his interests. It is by no means an easy matter to improve the esthetic standards of the retarded. Many of the characteristics seen in John's painting often more or less typify the work of the retarded. When a teacher has done his best in motivating and guiding the student, but becomes discouraged by the seeming lack of artistic development on the part of the pupil, he must seek solace in the fact that art is an educational avenue for self-development. The end purpose of art education does not lie solely in the production of beautiful art objects.

Figure 19. Steve, age 12, has drawn a picture of a time tunnel, having been motivated to depict a scene from the television program, "Time Tunnel." The question, "What do you think a time tunnel would look like?" inspired the artist to recall his favorite television program.

MOTIVATING THE RETARDED

Selection and Presentation of the Art Topic

Procedures for motivating the retarded to express themselves in art should be considered carefully. The educator's ability, or lack of ability, in motivating the retarded has a direct bearing on the success or failure of the child's creative art experience. The teacher must set the stage and prepare the way if meaningful art expressions are to unfold in the art classroom. The retarded cannot create in a vacuum. They must have ideas worthy of expression in art. When motivating the

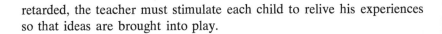

Figures 20 and 21. Larry, age 15, and brain damaged, conveys his conception of a tornado; Louis, age 16, a mongoloid, also illustrates his conception of a tornado. The students were dismissed early one day for a tornado watch; tornadoes then became the topic for an art experience the following day.

retarded, the teacher must stimulate each child to relive his experiences so that ideas are brought into play.

To motivate the retarded effectively, the teacher and children might together select an art topic which relates to the interests and experiences of the children. Two types of art topics could be considered: the *broad topic* and the *narrow topic*. The broad topic allows children to respond to the selected topic in many, diverse ways, whereas the narrow topic restricts children to the consideration of one event—one experience. The art topic, "My Favorite Sport," is an example of the broad topic. It allows children to respond in many ways. In discussing this theme, to be described in art, children might consider sports events which they have viewed as spectators, or sports activities in which they enjoy participating. The question, "What is your favorite sport?" might suggest the following subjects offered by the children: "The Football Game," "Playing Football," "The Boys' Baseball Game," "The Stockcar Races," "The Relay Race," "Roller Skating," etc. Each child is encouraged to respond to the broad topic with an idea of his own.

Figure 22. Mike, age 13 and brain damaged, was motivated to paint a picture of his home. The use of symbols recalls the work of a five- or six-year-old.

Figure 23 (below). Joe, age 11, a victim of brain damage, has colored a picture of his home. The heavy application of crayon results in a drawing which is bold and pronounced.

Figure 24 (right, above). Maris, age 15, a mongoloid, was motivated to create a seasonal drawing conveying signs of spring. Flowers, a warm sun and blue skies illustrate the season.

Figure 25 (right, below). Mike, age 14, has painted a picture of the family car.

The narrow topic, being more restrictive in nature, can be most effectively used to motivate children when it relates to a single event experienced commonly by all of the children. The class excursion, or field trip, provides one of the best opportunities to use the narrow topic. "Our Visit to the Fire Station" might be pursued in art by all children. Since the event was experienced by everyone, each child is able to relate to the confining theme in a meaningful, involved way.

In selecting a broad or narrow topic, the teacher should consider the criteria by which an effective topic is to be judged. An effective art topic must suggest mental images, and it must stimulate children to express these mental images in art. The topic must be personally meaningful, and it must relate to the interests of the retarded. If the experiences and interests of the children are ignored, the desire for expression will certainly not be kindled. Also, the topic should allow the retarded to be inventive in the exploration of their personal ideas. It is possible, in developing the topic, to over-motivate—to describe and discuss in too great detail the events relative to the broad or narrow theme. If too much is said, the student may rely upon his teacher for ideas, rather than exercising his imagination. In developing the theme, great detail and lengthy discussions should be avoided as the retarded are often able to grasp but a few ideas at one time. The exploration of many thoughts and ideas, relative to the chosen theme, may confuse the retarded child.

Once the topic has been chosen, the theme might be developed by means of questions asked by the teacher. The questions should relate to (1) activities associated with the selected theme, (2) the environment relating to the named activities, (3) the people involved in the mentioned activities, and sometimes (4) the bodily movements associated with the desired activity.

If the broad topic, "Our Favorite Sport Events," is chosen, the teacher will first want to establish which sport events are the favorites of each child. "What sport events do *you* most enjoy?" The teacher may not have time to listen to each child's response, but as children begin to respond to the question, others are listening and their minds will be stimulated. Next, the teacher will want to know where the sports events take place, i.e., the environment of the activity. "Where do you play baseball? Describe the baseball diamond. Are there large Coca-Cola signs in the background? Is there a wire fence behind the batter? Are there bleachers for the spectators? Describe all the details which can be seen on and around the ball diamond."

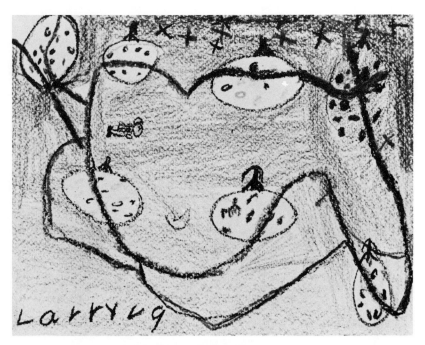

Figure 26.   Larry, age 15 and brain damaged, was motivated to depict an imaginary scene. The artist was invited to imagine objects one might see in outer space. Many flying saucers encircle the sky.

Now that the activity and its environment have been established and discussed, the players, the participants are now considered. "Whom do you wish to picture in your drawing? Who is playing baseball? Are you going to be in the drawing? Your friends? Would you prefer to show us the Detroit Tigers at play? What special uniforms would you or professionals wear? Describe the hats you might wear, the uniforms, the special shoes which would allow you to run fast."

Sometimes the mental image can be strengthened if body movements associated with the activity are discussed, described and pantomimed. "Suppose you stand beside your desk for a moment. Pretend you are batting the ball. How would you hold the bat? Swing your imaginary bat. Can you feel that the weight is on one leg, more than on the other? Will your arms be long enough to hold the bat? Can you feel how your whole body swings and turns when you swing the bat? Would someone like to show how a pitcher throws the ball? How would you describe the movements of the pitcher's body? Perhaps someone would like to show us the position of the catcher as he waits for the ball."

Art materials such as crayons, tempera paint or chalk should be distributed before the topic is discussed so that interest does not dwindle when the discussion has terminated. With materials at hand, the students are now ready to describe their chosen activity, environment, the participants and their actions.

In describing the development of the theme, "Our Favorite Sport Events," we should keep in mind that it might be necessary to shorten and abbreviate the discussion when motivating certain retarded children so as to avoid confusion. Sometimes it is necessary to narrow the discussion greatly so that only a few ideas are presented for consideration.

Sources for Art Topics

STORIES   There are a number of sources relative to retarded children's experiences which can be considered when selecting art topics for motivation. Children's stories, for example, provide a source of ideas which can be discussed prior to an art activity.

A story selected for the retarded is most effective when it stimulates the listener to identify with the actions of the story and the emotional feelings of the characters portrayed. Identification with the story may increase if the children are stimulated to dramatize a simple scene from the story which has been read by the teacher. An especially exciting part of the story might be selected for dramatization.

Also, identification with the actions and characters of the story is intensified when the teacher asks pertinent questions relating to a specific action, the environment in which this action takes place, the characters performing the action, and the manner in which the action takes place. Key questions beginning with the words *what* (action), *where* (environment), *who* (people, their activities, their physical appearance), and sometimes *how* (bodily demonstrations of action) will enrich mental images associated with the story.

Teachers of the retarded might also select a story which is unknown to the children and very exciting in terms of the described action. When reaching the most exciting part of the story, terminate the reading and invite the children to supply their own endings: "How do you think the story will end?" Invite children to draw and paint pictures which forecast the story's ending.

FIELD TRIPS   The class excursion provides one of the most effective ways of motivating the retarded to express themselves. Experiences are fresh in their memory during art class. Creative activities help the child to sum up his new experiences and think about them. He is drawn into a closer relationship with his environment. Relationships to the environment may become increasingly vital when the student is encouraged to dramatize verbally the experiences encountered on the class trip. When body movements accompany the verbal dramatization, ideas are further crystallized within the mind's eye.

Visits to the firehouse, post office, flower nursery, pet shop, zoo, aquarium or fruit market widen the retarded child's horizons and offer stimulating mental impressions which are realized in the art product. *Narrow topics* such as "Our Visit to the Fire House" or "Our Visit to the Pet Shop" effectively motivate children in art because each child can feel involved in the discussion. Each child has shared a common experience.

A mural relating to a field trip could be executed by a number of students. The planning of the mural may require organization much too difficult for the retarded. The proper relationships of size, color combinations and general layout of a mural may offer problems far too difficult for the retarded to comprehend. On the other hand, a mural which allows each child to work on his own separate part, these parts then being combined together in the last step, can result in a profitable experience for all. "Our Visit to the Fruit Market," for example, would allow each child to portray his own colorful booth containing clerks, scales, fruits, vegetables, flowers and customers. Each child should be encouraged to work on his own section of the long mural, painting or drawing upon uniformly sized sheets of paper. When finished, the papers of all children may be taped together (from behind) to formulate the long fruit market with its many booths drawn separately by each child.

SCRAP MATERIALS   A wide variety of scrap materials will go far in stimulating the retarded to express personal ideas in art. Scrap materials develop the child's sensitivity to texture. Arrange students in a circle and ask them to close their eyes. Distribute the scrap materials and ask them to pass them on to their neighbor after they have felt the materials. "What word might you use to describe the feel of the material? Does it feel rough? Smooth? Shiny? Jagged? Now open your eyes. This is the material you have felt. Let's feel another piece. Close your eyes again and tell me how the material feels in your hands."

"Now that we have felt different materials, let's construct a collage from them. If we are to make people, what kind of person would this paper doily suggest to you?"

"Cinderella, dressed for the ball."

"Very good. What person might you make out of this piece of burlap?"

"A lumberjack."

"Excellent! What does this colorful feather make you think of? A bird from the planet "X," perhaps? What art topics do these materials suggest to you?

"Perhaps some of you would like to make a non-representational collage, that is, a picture which does not show forms which we can recognize. If so, be sure to collect enough materials which have the same color and pattern so that you can cut them up and place them in various parts of your picture. Try to repeat the colors and patterns which are alike."

In preparation for art activities using titles suggested by scrap materials, ask children to collect old buttons, pieces of cloth, shells, macaroni, feathers, pie plates, wood scraps, string, toothpicks, tongue depressors, veiling, seeds, papers having different colors and textures, sequins and other materials.

PHONOGRAPH RECORDS Phonograph records provide yet another source for art topics for the purpose of motivation. Many recordings for children convey stories—both old and new—narrated by gifted actors and enlivened with sound effects and background music. Available commercial recordings for children may be found by consulting the *Schwann Supplementary Record Catalog* published in Spring and Fall editions by W. Schwann, Inc., 137 Newbury Street, Boston, Massachusetts 02116. The supplementary catalog is available from most record stores throughout the United States.

Among the records suitable for motivating the retarded in art, and listed in the Schwann Supplementary Catalog, are

- Animal Song Parade—Harmony 9516
- Best Loved Fairy Tales—Disneyland 1918
- Bozo at the Circus—Capitol JAO 3259
- Casper, the Friendly Ghost—Golden 8017
- Cinderella—Disneyland 3908
- Mary Poppins: Songs and Story—Disneyland 3922
- Peter Pan—Disneyland 3910
- Wizard of Oz—Golden 13

After the children have heard the record, a brief discussion should follow—a discussion which emphasizes a few of the activities conveyed in the story. Lengthy discussions and the presentation of too many ideas only confuse the retarded child, and leave him with no clear ideas for expression in art.

IMAGINARY OCCUPATIONS The topic, "What I Want to Be When I Grow Up," enables retarded children to identify with the adult world and to think of occupations they might wish to pursue. In a world providing few opportunities for leadership, the retarded commonly imagine themselves in positions of authority—thereby expressing their desire to succeed. A discussion relating to occupations provides excellent opportunity to discuss the unique environment of a specific occupation, to consider special uniforms which are worn on the job, and to mentally describe specific activities carried out in a chosen occupation.

SCIENCE The study of science—a look to nature—can provide and suggest topics well suited for motivating children in art. Take students on a "looking walk" in search of interesting objects such as colorful stones, berries, colored leaves or symmetrical insects. Observe the colors, shapes and textures of butterflies, caterpillars, ladybugs. Encourage children to create large drawings and paintings based on their new-found knowledge.

Invite children to take magnifying glasses on their "looking walk." Objects from nature take on an enlarged view—calling attention to detail. Art expressions will reflect the magnified view in a most interesting way. Children will be encouraged to enlarge their drawings when the topic is "Our View Through the Magnifying Glass."

Keep a "nature box" in the classroom and invite children to contribute objects of beauty. When a number of items have been collected, distribute them. Invite children to handle the objects—to feel their texture and shape—to examine their color, and to create imaginative drawings and paintings inspired by their observations.

Self Portraits: Improving the Body Image

Normal children, at the age of four, five and sometimes as late as six years, begin to depict the human figure in their drawings for the first time. The retarded child may greatly delay his representation of the human figure until reaching a more advanced chronological age—remaining, meanwhile, in the scribbling stage. Scribbled lines and random strokes may characterize the retarded child's art work until the age of seven and far beyond. During the later stages of the scribbling stage the retarded may title their scribblings. Titles may make reference to the human form: "This is Mamma," "This is me." The child may link scribbled lines with figures and imaginative experiences. But the actual realization of these figures is related to a later stage in the retarded child's development.

Teachers and parents should not interfere with the scribblings of retarded children. Children are inhibited when teachers try to force them to make recognizable forms. The retarded should be encouraged to continue their random movements in an atmosphere of complete freedom.

Art topics should come from the retarded child during the later phases of the scribbling stage, and not from the teacher. The teacher motivates the child only after a subject is suggested by the child. The child might say, "This is me kicking a ball." To stimulate imaginative activity, the teacher or parent might respond by saying, "Show me your ball. How do you kick the ball? Can you show me?" The child's thinking and feeling processes are directed by the adult as the scribbling activity unfolds.

When the first symbol for the human figure appears in the art work of the retarded, it is usually geometric in form: a circle represents the head; vertical lines suggest the body. This geometric concept changes from time to time as the search for the complete symbol progresses.

Enrichment of the figure occurs when the teacher activates the thought processes of children by providing new and individual experiences. Meaningful experiences cause children to increase their knowledge of their subject, so that passive knowledge of the figure becomes active. The degree to which the child enriches his concept of the human form is contingent upon his mental abilities and also upon his ability to react emotionally to the motivational procedures employed by the classroom teacher.

Figures 27 through 38 show portrait and figure drawings by retarded children whose mental ages rarely measured above 5 or 6 years, but whose chronological ages were as high as 13, 14 and above. In many instances the drawings closely resemble the work of normal children whose chronological and mental ages might range from 4 to 5. The geometric symbols representing the human form are very much in evidence.

Figure 27 (facing page). Students were motivated to enrich the self image by drawing a self portrait. Attention was called to details such as the hair, eyes, mouth and nose. John, age 13 (mental age 4.5), filled his paper with eight figures, relating them to actual persons in the audience.

Figure 28 (above). Mark, age 14 (M. A. 3.3), included many figures in his drawing.

Figure 29 (below). Carol, age 14, M. A. 2.7, was unable to relate to the discussion. Scribbles characterize her work.

Figure 30. Terry, age 14, also had difficulty relating to the assigned art topic. Carol and Terry might be withheld from future organized art lessons until some further stage in their development.

Figure 31.   Karla, C. A. 14, M. A. 4.5, ignored the idea of drawing a self-portrait and depicted instead her favorite television personality.

In motivating these children, I wanted to increase their awareness of the self, especially the head and its features. I asked one child to step before the class to serve as a model. Calling attention to the model's head, I asked the students to describe the shape of the head. I asked them to use a word to describe the shape of the head; thinking they might use such terms as "oval" or "circle." These terms seemed to hold little or no meaning for the children. Consequently, I asked them to trace their hands around their own faces, to feel the shape of the oval. Once the nature of the shape was realized, we proceeded to discuss the facial features. "Where are the eyes located within the oval?" Observing the model, students learned that the eyes were located in the center. Further questions brought forth the realization that the nose was located vertically between the eyes and chin, and that the ears were located in line with the eyes and nose. Students were now invited to draw portraits of themselves. I circulated about the room and offered comments relative to the children's work, praising them for the inclusion of detail. Often I would mention details aloud, to remind other students of features they might wish to include. "Mark has drawn dark black hair on the top of his head. Mary has the most beautiful buttons drawn on her dress. Karla has added a most interesting collar about the neck." These comments served to activate the imaginations of other children to some extent. Some students offered very few details, as their stage of mental development did not enable them to grasp the many ideas set forth. In motivating some children it is wise to discuss only a few ideas at a time to avoid confusion.

John, age 13, with a mental age of 4.5 and an I.Q. of 45, enjoyed the drawing activity immensely. Figure 27 reveals that John has filled his paper with eight figures, all of which are similar in character. While drawing, John observed the adult audience of college students, teachers and principal, and announced that he was creating life-like representations of various members of the audience who had assembled to view the drawing activity. When finished, he pointed to one figure in the drawing and proclaimed it was his principal. He asked her to observe his rendition of her hair. Next he pointed to other members, informing them where they were located within the drawing. To John, his figures definitely represented certain people present, but his drawing shows figures which are too similar in detail to describe individual differences of the people present. John was extremely outgoing and he verbalized greatly about his art work, captivating the audience as he worked.

Mark, age 14, with a mental age of 3.3 and an I.Q. of 35, also included many figures within his drawing (Figure 28). You will notice that our discussion motivated Mark to place the eyes within the vertical center of the circular face. The idea of adding buttons to the clothing fascinated the young artist. His rendition of hair is similar for all figures. Observe the geometric nature of the human schema as realized during this child's early stage of artistic development.

For the sake of contrast, it is interesting to compare the work of a child having a younger mental age than that of John or Mark. Carol, age 14, with a mental age of 2.7, was unable to relate to the discussion and procedures of motivation. Her scribbles (Figure 29) reveal that she is not yet ready to produce the human schema within her drawing, and it would have been to the child's advantage to exclude her from the drawing activity herewith described. At this stage of development, topics should not be assigned.

Terry, age 14 (see Figure 30), also had difficulty relating to the assigned art topic and should probably be eliminated from structured group activities until the scribbling stage is replaced by the schematic stage, as evidenced by the appearance of the human figure.

Maris, age 15, gives us a surprising account of the human figure when we consider that he has a mental age of 2. The discussion motivated Maris to include hair, a beard, and buttons upon his shirt (Figure 31).

MARISDAINIS

Figures 32 to 34. Left, Maris, age 15, included hair, a beard, and buttons upon his shirt. Center, Beverly, C. A. 13, M. A. 3.2, has drawn a figure which reveals that the human schema has just begun to develop in her art work. The geometric nature of the figure and the lack of detail reveal Beverly's early stage of development. Right, Herman, C. A. 16, M. A. 5.9, experienced difficulty in relating to the chosen theme. The figure is small and cramped, revealing little detail.

Karla, C.A. 14, M.A. 4.5, chose to ignore the idea of creating a self-portrait, and has, instead, created a clown named "Bozo," inspired by a figure frequently seen on local television. The eyes are typically placed high within the circular head. Figure 32 shows imagination, especially when one considers her stage of development.

Beverly, C.A. 13, M.A. 3.2, has drawn a figure (Figure 33) which reveals that the human schema has just begun to develop in her art work. The geometric nature of the figure and the lack of detail reveal Beverly's early stage of mental development.

Herman, C.A. 16, M.A. 5.9, experienced difficulty in relating to the chosen theme. Figure 34 is small and cramped, revealing little detail.

Mike, C.A. 14, M.A. 5.9, gives us an unusual portrait in Figure 35, in that we have a side view of the face. This interpretation does not typify children's usual interpretations of the face, and Mike's portrait is in contrast to the position taken by the model during our discussion of the facial features. But the approach is most welcome in that it reveals that Mike is able to move beyond the described idea for the sake of a personal interpretation. Mike's rendition of hair and sideburns gives further evidence of his unique abilities to perceive.

Other interpretations of the self are revealed in the drawings of Milo, C.A. 14, M.A. 6.6, Figure 36; Bruce, C.A. 17, M.A. 6.2, Figure 37; and Sandy, C.A. 14, I.Q. 47, Figure 38.

Figure 35 (right). Mike, C. A. 14, M. A. 5.9, has drawn an unusual portrait in that we see a side view of the face.

Figures 36, 37 and 38 (facing page). Other interpretations of the self are revealed in the drawings of Milo (C. A. 14, M. A. 6.6), Bruce (C. A. 17, M. A. 6.2) and Sandy (C. A. 14, I. Q. 47).

Art Appreciation

Many teachers of the retarded recognize that art appreciation is often ineffective in strengthening the imaginative powers of the retarded. Visits to the local art galleries seem to leave the students rather cold. They are unable to draw from their past experiences in identifying with the theme of a painting. In some instances the simpler, more primitive art forms allow for greater self-identification. Primitive Eskimo carvings, Indian carvings and handcrafts may come closer to the retarded child's way of thinking and working. The retarded can identify better with the style and general theme of a painting by such a primitive artist as the late Grandma Moses than with the abstract works of such artists as Kandinski, Marin or Picasso.

EVALUATION OF THE ART PRODUCT

Each child sets his own standard in art, and each child's work must be evaluated in relationship to himself, not other members of the class. Art is a very personal expression of the inner self. Art is an avenue for expression of feelings, experiences, moods and ideas. How can we declare that the experiences, feelings and moods of one child are more legitimate or worthy than those of another? Number or letter grades, which would compare artistic performances for each child with those of his classmates, should be avoided. Nor should the work of the retarded be compared with that of average children.

Periodically, examples of children's art work should be saved and kept in a folder so that the progress of each child may be observed. In comparing the child's work with previous expressions, it is interesting to note if a greater coordination between hand and eye is evident in the manipulation of art tools. Also, the teacher will wish to observe whether more detail is evident in each child's art expressions. Is the child growing in his awareness of his environment? A study of the child's representation of the human schema will reveal much concerning his growth. Are arms and legs and detail nearly always included? Are the figures stiff and stereotyped, or varied in their posture and movements? Is the child beginning to differentiate between boys and girls in conveying detail? Answers to these questions can provide insights into creative and mental growth when art expressions of each child are observed.

The artistic expressions of the retarded will often appear crude, showing little or no concern for design principles. Teachers must learn to accept honest art expressions of the retarded, rather than try to enforce adult rules which will guarantee predescribed, sophisticated, adult-like performances. The value of creative art experiences for the retarded lies in the act of creation, not the creation of beautiful art examples which please the adult.

Evaluating the Teacher's Performance

A teacher's performance as a teacher of art may be evaluated as the retarded child's art expressions are observed. If the art projects of retarded children are similar in construction, shape and color, one must conclude that the artistic ideas are those of the teacher, not the children. If individuality in expression is evident, it would appear the teacher is allowing the retarded to think for themselves, to make their own decisions, to express their own ideas. And here lies the value of art: if creatively taught, art can foster independence in thinking.

Figure 39.   A make-believe television set may be an aid in stimulating the child with retarded speech development to speak about his art product.

SPECIAL TECHNIQUES, METHODS AND MATERIALS

Television Displays

The mentally retarded often experience a somewhat delayed or limited development of speech. Children should not feel that the drawing of a picture is a substitute for speech. When possible, the child should be encouraged to talk about his art work. The make-believe television set (Figure 39) may be an aid in stimulating the child to gain freedom in his ability to speak. To make this set, a large hole the shape of a TV picture tube is cut into the bottom of a corrugated cardboard box. When set on its side, the bottom then becomes the front or picture area of the TV. A sheet of cardboard, the size of the front area, is placed inside the set so that it lies directly behind the picture-tube opening. A strip of paper tape, pasted along the bottom of this cardboard, turns the cardboard into a flap which can be shoved backwards or forwards against the inner front of the set. The student may push the flap backwards, place his painting on it, and then push the flap forward so that the painting is pressed between the flap and the front of the set. He now becomes a television announcer as he talks about his painting. Spools or cardboard tubes may be placed below the picture area for dials. If the student speaks too softly when discussing his painting, the teacher may ask him to turn up the volume knob. This device, if not overused, can be effective in helping the child lose his inhibitions as he speaks before the class. The teacher should use discretion in choosing paintings for discussion. Some works of art may not be storytelling pictures. If forced to talk about such a painting, the child may feel he has been most inadequate in his artistic expression. The making and handling of puppets offers another most effective avenue for verbal expression. The student literally "loses himself" when speaking for his inanimate friend.

Demonstrations

The handling of art materials and the teaching of techniques for using them provides the teacher with many a challenge. The introduction of a new material may excite little interest in the child. The teacher may have to employ the closure method, i.e., an experience begun by the teacher and finished by the child. Teacher may form a ball of clay into the shape of a head. She will then ask, "Where do you think the eyes ought to be? The ears?" When the child has become more secure in using clay, he should be encouraged to create objects completely of his own invention.

It takes the retarded child a longer period of time to fully explore the possibilities of his art materials. Learning takes place when repetition is not carried too far. There is the danger however, that the repetitious use of materials and related techniques may bring about a standstill in the creative development of the child. If such is the case, the teacher may have to encourage the child to seek new ways of using his materials. She may have to hold the child's hand over a crayon and demonstrate how various hand movements result in dissimilar effects. If the older child persists in using the same paintbrush and color, the teacher may want to remove both articles so that the student is forced to explore new tools and colors.

Teacher demonstrations of materials and techniques must be carefully geared to the creative needs of the student. A more detailed demonstration is required for the retarded than would be necessary, say, for the gifted. However, it is possible to reveal so much in a demonstration that the retarded really have little chance to make discoveries on thir own. Enough should be said to stimulate interest in using a new material or process and to provide a measure of security in proceeding on one's own, but comment should be limited so as not to stifle the creative energies of the child. The teacher must carefully search out the needs of his students.

In teaching the retarded, the instructor is perhaps most greatly tempted to involve his students in "accidental" art activities in order to produce pleasing, sophisticated results. It is not uncommon to find the retarded dropping a string upon the surface of a paper and then coloring in the shapes accidentally made by the string. Such tricks or gimmicks could be of value if the retarded capitalized on the results and worked beyond the accidental stage. But such is usually not the case. The technique becomes an end in itself. The how-to-do-it techniques fool the student into thinking he has achieved something quite beautiful, when actually he has had no part in being original or creative. The ideas are the teacher's, and the children simply parrot them. Mental development is not fostered. The child is not given the chance to react to his environment in his own unique way. Emotional feelings remain dormant. Such practices have little educational value in the training of the retarded.

Printing Techniques

The various printing processes have been found to offer many a rewarding artistic activity for the retarded. These processes include vegetable printing; finger and hand printing; gadget printing; yarn, string or pipe cleaner printing; tin can printing; stencil printing; mono-printing; linoleum, wood, plaster of Paris, paraffin and soap printing; and inner tube, cardboard and string printing. The process of printing, which is relatively uncomplicated, and the gratifying results both serve to meet the artistic needs of the retarded.

SIMPLE TECHNIQUES   The young retarded child will enjoy finger and hand printing (Figures 40 and 41). The thumb, fingertips and other parts of the hand are dipped into the ink and used to print various shapes and designs.

Figure 40. The various printing processes have been found to offer many rewarding artistic activities for the retarded. The simplest printing techniques are those which do not require carving, cutting or gluing. *Finger printing* falls into this category. Fingers are pressed onto an inked glass and then onto paper to create a design. In this example, Jackie (C. A. 8, M. A. 7) has printed a picture of her home.

Figure 41 (facing page). In *finger and hand printing*, the finger tips, knuckles, palm and side of the hand are dipped in ink and pressed upon paper to create a variety of effects. John (C. A. 9, M. A. 8) has printed a violent scene upon colored tissue paper. A man's figure (seen at the extreme left) is fleeing from a burning building.

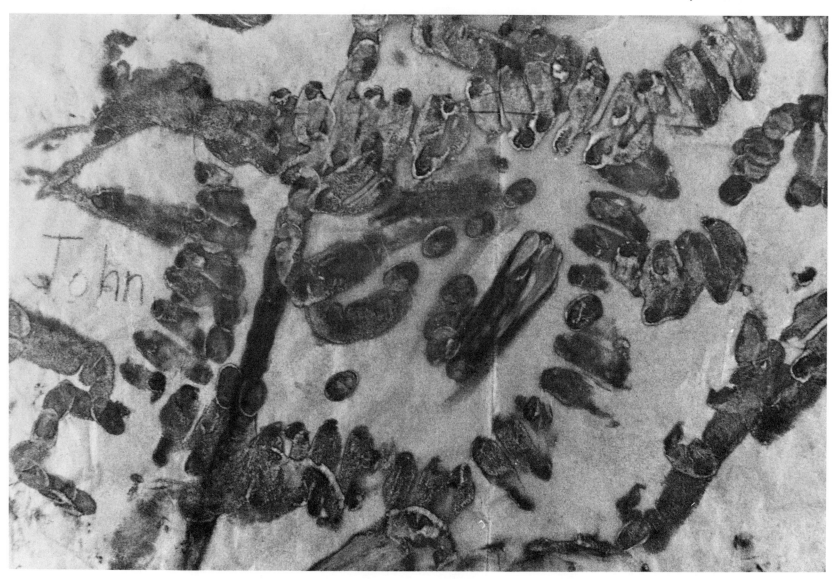

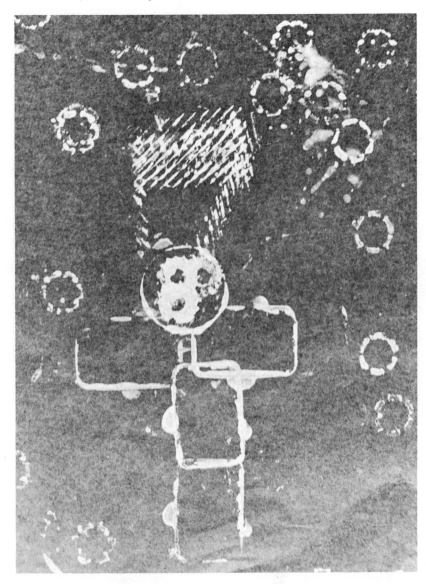

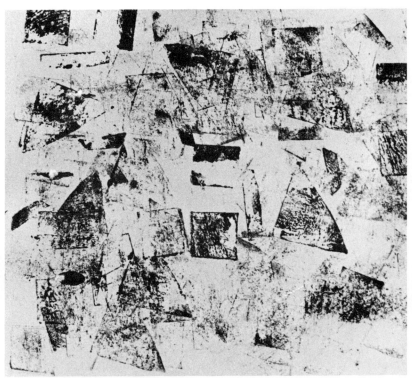

Figure 43 (above). *Wood scrap printing* is another simple technique. Scrap pieces of wood (available free from most lumber yards) are used in printing. Imagine the interesting shapes achieved by using the ends of various moldings. And visualize the interesting textures one might achieve with the grain of the wood, or the sawed end of a piece of wood. In this example, Kris (C. A. 15.4, I. Q. 71) has created a variety of shapes and textures with her wood scraps.

Figure 42 (left). *Gadget printing* is another example of a simple printing technique which does not require cutting and gluing. Gadgets such as clothespins, wooden spools, empty pill boxes and kitchen items are pressed onto the inked glass and then onto paper. In this example Jeff (C. A. 10, M. A. 8) has pressed various gadgets onto a sheet of colored tissue paper.

Gadget printing also meets the needs of the younger child. Common articles, such as spools or scrap wood blocks, are used to print and repeat various forms (Figures 42 and 43). Another simple technique is clay printing, shown in Figures 44 and 45.

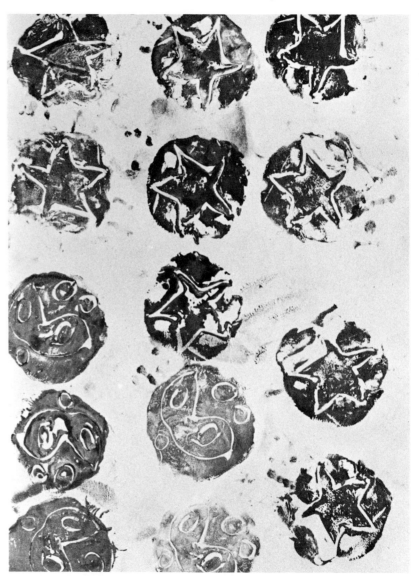

Figures 44 and 45. *Clay printing* affords another simple printing technique. A piece of oil-based clay is shaped into the desired form. The eraser or the point of a pencil and other gadgets may be poked into the clay to create interesting patterns and textures. After the printing procedure, the clay is held under the water faucet to rinse away the water-soluble printer's ink. The ball of clay is now reshaped, and the printing procedure continues. Below, Carl (C. A. 13.10) has pressed the initials "M. J." into his piece of clay. Right, Robert (C. A. 15.8, I. Q. 70) has imprinted stars and various free forms into his piece of clay before printing.

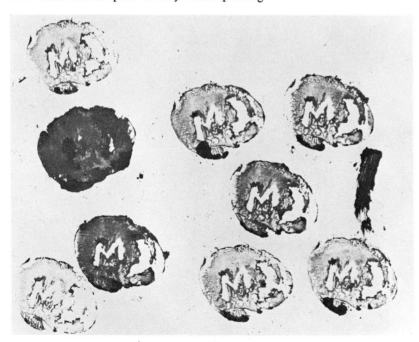

SUBTRACTIVE METHOD   In vegetable printing (Figures 46-48), the young artist may use a potato, onion, carrot, etc.   The vegetable can be sliced into two parts, each having a flat surface.   A knife is used to cut away the parts of the surface which are not to leave an imprint upon paper.   A brayer is used to spread water-soluble printer's ink or a mixture of tempera paint and liquid starch upon a glass surface; the vegetable is then pressed upon the inked glass surface, raised and pressed against a sheet of absorbent paper many times, creating a repetitious design of pleasing beauty.   A brush may be used to apply the paint to the vegetable, thus eliminating the need for a brayer or glass.

Printing with linoleum, wood, plaster of Paris, paraffin or soap is similar to vegetable printing in that recessed areas are cut away from a flat surface.   The raised areas which have not been cut away are repeatedly inked and pressed against paper or cloth.   Special carving tools are usually needed in making a linoleum or wood block print; battle linoleum and the softer woods are most suitable for use.

Figure 46.   In the *subtractive method* for printing, a flat surface is used and parts are carved or cut away.   The remaining portions of the surface are inked and pressed onto paper.   *Potato printing* is an example of the subtractive method.   Carl (C. A. 13.10) has created an interesting repeated design with his potato.

ADDITIVE METHOD   In this method, parts are not cut away from a surface but are *added* to a flat surface, such as a block of wood or Masonite. The applied materials may be such things as cardboard (Figures 49 and 50), pipe cleaners (Figure 51), yarn (Figure 52), string or pieces of innertube. A coat of shellac will prevent these materials from coming off the wood block when it is soaked with water-soluble ink. The block is inked in the manner described for vegetable printing. Pipe cleaners are especially effective in printing lines of interesting texture and beauty.

Tin can printing (Figures 53 and 54) involves the gluing of string, felt, etc. to the outside surface of the can. When inked, the can is rolled over a long sheet of paper. The seam of the tin can makes an effective guide for beginning and ending each section of the long continuous print.

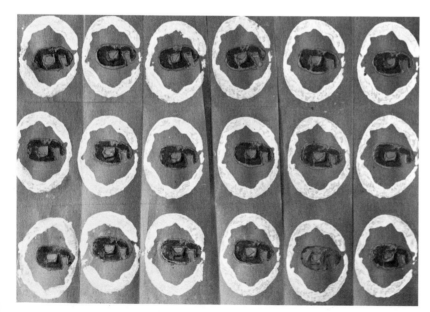

Figure 47.   Two potatoes were used in this work. One was used to create the white circle, and a second potato was carved to form the figure "6" seen in the center of each motif.

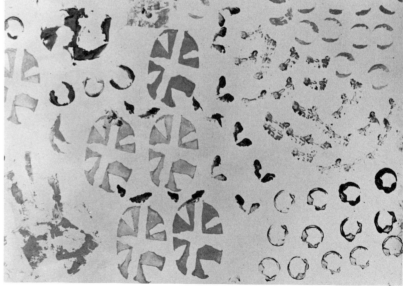

Figure 48.   This may best be described as an example of *vegetable printing*, which combines the subtractive method (potato printing) with simpler methods. A potato and the ends of celery stalks and carrots were used by Debbie (C. A. 10.9, I. Q. 68) to create this design.

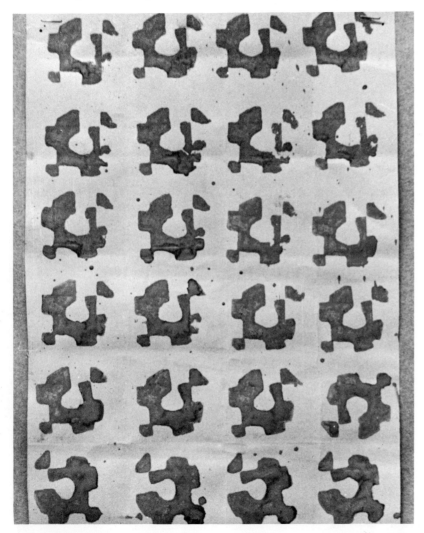

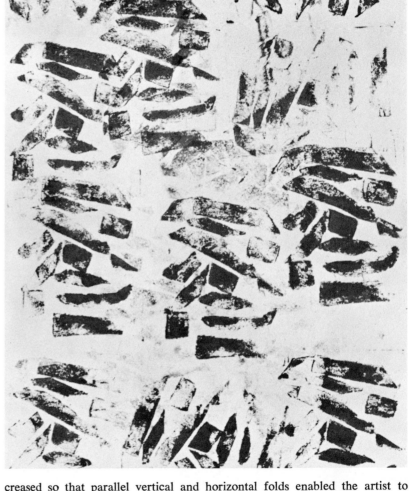

Figures 49 and 50.   In the additive method sections are not cut away from a flat surface; instead, shapes are added to a flat surface.   In *cardboard printing*, interesting shapes are cut from cardboard and glued onto the flat side of a piece of wood.   In Figure 49 (left), the background paper was creased so that parallel vertical and horizontal folds enabled the artist to organize his cardboard printing more neatly.   In Figure 50 (right), Kim (C. A. 15, I. Q. 67) glued small pieces of cardboard onto wood and printed a repeat design upon construction paper of a contrasting color.

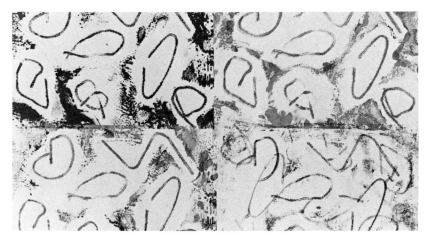

Figure 51. *Pipe cleaner printing* is another example of the additive method. Non-water soluble glue is used, so that the pipe cleaners will not fall off the wood block when moistened with the printer's ink. Danny (C. A. 13.3, M. A. 9) has created an interesting repeat design by pressing his woodblock and pipe cleaners four times on construction paper.

Figure 53. *Tin can printing* is another additive method. Various objects, such as string, yarn, cord, felt pieces or ribbed corrugated cardboard, are glued onto a tin can. The protruding pieces are inked and the can is rolled over paper, leaving the printed design. Joe (C. A. 12.8, I. Q. 76) has glued a variety of materials onto a coffee can to create his design.

Figure 52. *Yarn printing* affords another approach for using the additive method in printing, as in this example by Dawn (C. A. 8, M. A. 7).

Figure 54. Pieces of felt were glued to a tin can in this example of tin can printing by Steve (C. A. 16.4, I. Q. 79).

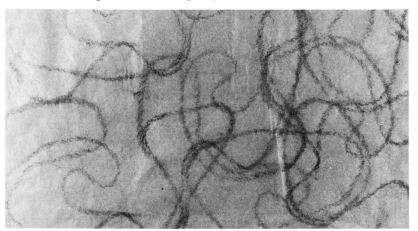

OTHER METHODS   Some printing techniques can hardly be called simple, nor do they fit the description of the additive or subtractive methods.   In *relief printing* (Figure 55), flat, textured forms cut from mesh vegetable bags, cardboard and other materials are placed beneath a sheet of flat paper, such as newsprint. A brayer is inked and run over newspaper to remove most of the ink. With just a little ink left on the brayer, the tool is run over the newsprint, thereby revealing the shape and texture of the cut object(s) below.

In *stencil printing* (Figures 56 and 57), the student cuts away various shapes from non-absorbent, sturdy paper such as tagboard.   Thinner papers oiled with cooking oil may also be used, provided they do not tear during the printing process.   Interesting "windows" are cut into the paper and a brayer or sponge is used to apply ink to the surface of the stencil, thus leaving an imprint upon paper or cloth where the areas have been cut from the stencil.

A monoprint is made by placing a sheet of absorbent paper upon the inked surface of glass.   A pencil and other gadgets are used to draw upon the top side of the paper, thus creating an inked impression on the reverse side.   The same paper may be laid upon various inked glass surfaces to produce a variety of colors.   Best results are obtained when the ink is allowed to become rather tacky.

Figure 55.   Sue (C. A. 15.4, I. Q. 71) has placed rectangular shapes cut from cardboard beneath a sheet of newsprint to create her relief print.

Figures 56 and 57.   Cindy (C. A. 12.10, I. Q. 70) has used a modification of the stencil technique to create two peace symbols.   Ink was rolled onto the stencil and the stencil was then applied to paper, inked side down, both to make the stencil stick and to leave color on the paper.   While the stencil was still in place, Cindy rolled another color over the negative areas.   When the stencil was peeled off, two colors were left.

Metal Tooling

COPPER TOOLING   The tooling of metal such as copper and aluminum provides the retarded with many opportunities to create art objects which they can be proud of. The finished product is nearly always pleasing to the eye.

In introducing this technique, the teacher must be certain that his students have the necessary physical dexterity. In working with some students, it might be wise to limit the tooling process to approximately twenty minutes. Two or three brief periods per day or week are less taxing than one long period.

Copper is available from most arts and crafts stores in rolls which may easily be cut into small pieces with scissors. Cut pieces measuring approximately six by ten inches provide a suitable working area for most children.

To begin, invite children to draw a preliminary design upon newsprint, identical in size to the copper sheet. A scribble drawing (Figure 58) will afford one approach to planning the design. Instruct children to place their pencils on the paper so as to create one continuous line which overlaps, runs off the edge of the paper, comes back onto the paper, continues across the paper, etc., until a design is created which has shapes that vary in size. Encourage children to vary the shapes and sizes.

In planning their designs, some children may wish to draw floral designs. To motivate them, invite them to pretend that they are small birds searching for beautiful flowers. As they fly through the sky, lovely flowers are suddenly seen below. "Some of the flowers are large. Others are small. Do you suppose the flowers are surrounded by leaves? Stems? What might your blossoms look like when viewed from above? What do you see in the center of your blossom? How many petals does it have?" Once again, through discussion, students learn that for the sake of a pleasing design, shapes should vary in size.

"How many blossoms shall we place within our design? Perhaps we should have at least two or three so that we are able to *repeat* our shapes."

When completed, the design is placed over the sheet of copper, with a few sheets of newspaper beneath the copper sheet for padding. Using a pencil, the lines of the drawn design are redrawn, causing the line design to be embossed on the copper sheet below.

Students are now ready to tool their copper sheets. They must decide which of the shapes are to be raised and which to be lowered. The *raised shapes* are tooled (or rubbed) with a tongue depressor, sucker stick, or the handle of a spoon from the reverse side of the copper sheet. All *lowered shapes* are rubbed along the front side of the copper sheet. The copper sheet, then, is tooled from both sides, depending upon whether the shapes are to be raised or lowered.

Once the tooling process is completed, students are ready to add patterns and textures. Many students like to stipple in their patterns, using the point of a nail. Others might wish to draw parallel lines or crossed parallel lines with a sharp instrument. Circles, wavy lines, scalloped lines, squares or triangles might be densely drawn upon the copper when creating patterns. Invite children to leave some areas plain (especially the raised shapes) so that the design does not become too busy—too complicated. In Figure 59 you will note that crossed parallel lines were drawn in the low shapes whereas stippled dots were applied, from the reverse side, to the raised shapes.

Next, the copper must be oxidized with a solution of liver of sulphur (potassium sulfide), which can be ordered through your local drug store. A few lumps are dissolved in a water-filled peanut butter jar and applied to the copper with a sponge. The sulphur application will immediately turn the copper black. When dry, the copper is rubbed with steel wool, thus antiqueing the surface. The rubbing process causes the raised areas to appear bright and light, offering a pleasing contrast to the darker low areas. A final coating of clear shellac or varnish will prevent the oxidized areas from turning a chalky gray color.

When dry, the copper is ready to be mounted. Using Elmer's glue, the copper may be applied to a sheet of tagboard which is glued to a larger sheet of black construction paper. Sheets of cork likewise provide an interesting frame, as do pieces of wood which have an attractive grain. Decorative upholstery tacks provide a most interesting border when nailed around the edge of the copper, into the wood.

Copper tooling introduces the retarded to a few simple considerations relating to a pleasing design. And the technique intensifies an awareness of texture.

ALUMINUM TOOLING   The technique of tooling aluminum is almost identical with that of copper tooling, except that India ink is used to blacken the aluminum instead of the sulphur, which will not oxidize .aluminum. Before the aluminum is painted with India ink, it should be bathed in ammonia water and lightly rubbed with steel wool so as to remove all oily finger prints which could cause the ink to resist the aluminum surface. When dry, the inked surface is rubbed with steel wool in the manner described for copper.

Aluminum pie plates and other food containers can be used in tooling aluminum. The rims of the plates may be cut away, or left on when tooling an ash tray. The aluminum process enables the retarded to work with materials which in most cases are free.

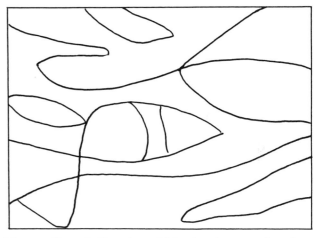

Figures 58 and 59. A scribble drawing transferred to copper. The artist must decide which of the shapes will be tooled so that they rise upward; other shapes will be tooled so that they recede. In the tooled copper, parallel line patterns were drawn onto the lower shapes. A dot pattern, located in the raised shapes, was stippled onto the reverse side.

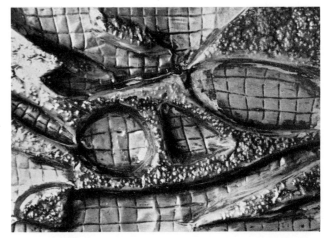

Paper Sculpture

Construction paper is one of the most economical and readily available materials for the art program. Construction paper, combined wtih collected scrap paper materials, provides avenues for varied explorations in art which are meaningful to the retarded.

Papers which may be combined with and applied to construction paper include poster paper, metallic foil, colored tissue, gift wrapping paper, newspaper (particularly the want-ad sections), Japanese origami papers, tag board, magazine paper, cellophane, paper towels, napkins, cardboard, stationery, sandpaper and wallpaper.

BASIC FORMS   There are four basic forms which should be demonstrated when the retarded are ready to explore the possibilities of paper sculpture. The *cone* is constructed by cutting a circle from paper. A slit is cut from the edge of the circle to the exact center. The resulting edges are overlapped and glued, thus forming the cone.

The *cylinder* is simple to construct. A rectangular sheet of paper is curled, and the opposite ends are joined with glue or brass paper fasteners.

The *cube* may be constructed like a cylinder, except that three creases are folded into the paper so that the resulting form has four sides.

The *triangle* is likewise constructed from a rectangular sheet of paper which has two parallel creases. Opposite ends of the paper are joined together.

Figure 60.   One fold in a sheet of paper, located along the back, enables a paper sculptured animal to stand.   Scott (C. A. 11.7, I. Q. 71) has created a furry monofold animal.

CONNECTING MATERIALS   The four basic forms may be joined together in any kind of combination to create people, animals, free forms, houses, flowers, etc. Connecting materials, which hold the basic forms together, include staples, transparent tape, white library paste, Elmer's glue, rubber cement, masking tape, rubber bands, paper clips, pins and brass paper fasteners.

SCRAP DECORATIVE MATERIALS   Having constructed objects by using the basic forms, the retarded will next enjoy decorating the objects with collected scrap materials. A generous supply of scrap materials will enliven the surfaces of any paper sculptured form. "How might we use these paper cups? Could they be attached for a nose or hat? Would these paper straws add interest to your paper form? Could they be used as animal whiskers? Hair? Thin arms and legs? Would the shiny ribbon enhance the skirt or blouse of our figures? Perhaps twine could be unraveled and used for hair. This lace might make a perfect trim for the sleeves of a paper figure."

Scrap materials might include wood scraps, wooden blocks, TV dinner trays, toothpicks, tongue depressors, straw, stove pipe wire, plastic "spaghetti" tubing, pipe cleaners, pieplates, paper tubes, paper doilies, paper cups, paper bags, milk containers, match sticks, mailing tubes, lollipop sticks, lace, ice cream sticks, flash bulbs, egg cartons, corn husks, corks, cloth, cardboard rollers and boxes, bell wire.

MONOFOLD FORMS: *Animals*   Monofold forms provide one of the simplest techniques for constructing three-dimensional objects from paper. One fold is made, and the flat sheet suddenly takes on the third dimension. "What might we make from this folded sheet of paper which stands by itself? An animal would be easy to make." Figure 60 reveals that the fold of the paper is at the animal's back. By cutting through both thicknesses of the folded sheet, an animal is constructed which will stand on four legs. Scott (C.A. 11.7, I.Q. 71) glued yarn to the sides of his monofold animal to suggest fur (Figure 60).

People   People are easy to construct, using the monofold technique. In Figure 61, the trousers of the male figure are illustrated. The fold, you will notice, is located along the waist of the figure. In Figure 62 a two-dimensional top section has been glued onto the three-dimensional trousers, and the figure now stands by itself.

Figure 63 shows that the female figure is constructed in much the same way—the fold of the paper is located at the waist.

Examples of monofold people may be seen in Figures 64 and 65. Figure 64 shows how scrap materials can be used to decorate the form: a curled wood shaving provides hair, with braided yarn serving as pigtails. Buttons are glued down for eyes. A pipe cleaner serves as a smiling mouth. Various pieces of patterned and plain cloth are glued in place for the blouse, tie and skirt. Felt pieces are used for the red shoes.

Figure 61 (below).   For the male monofold figure, the paper is folded at the waist.

Figure 62 (right).   A two-dimensional top section is added and the figure is complete.

Figure 63 (far right).   For the female monofold form, also, the fold is located at the waist.

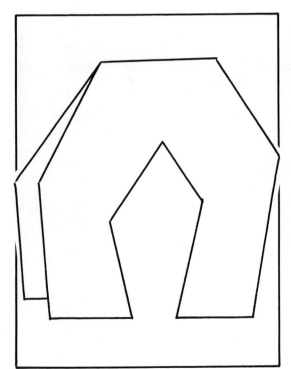

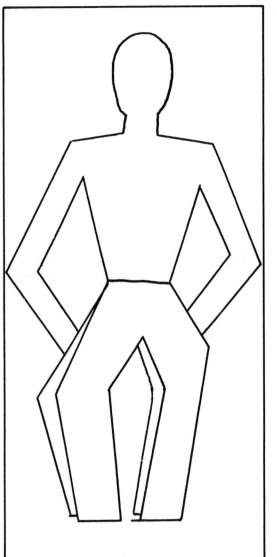

Figure 64.   A number of scrap materials decorate the monofold person by Carl (C. A. 10.9, I. Q. 68).

In Figure 65, at the left, Debbie (C.A. 10.9, I.Q. 68) has used colorful bits of patterned cloth for the clothes.   Large sequins serve as shiny shoes, and braided yarn hangs in pigtails.   The right-hand figure, by Joe (C.A. 12.8, I.Q. 76), displays colorful stripes of ric-rac, with ribbon added for the belt.

Figure 65.   Bits of cloth, yarn, sequins and ric-rac decorate the two monofold people in the examples by Debbie (C. A. 10.9, I. Q. 68), seen to the left, and by Joe (C. A. 12.8, I. Q. 76), as seen to the right.

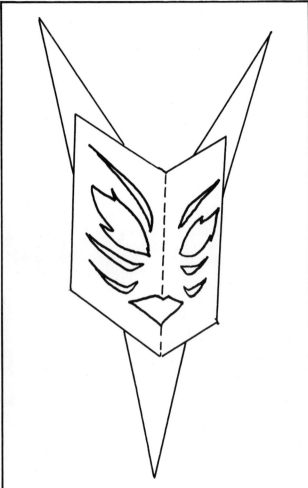

Figure 66. One vertical fold in a sheet of paper enables the artist to create a symmetrical monofold mask. Scrap materials and paper-sculpture forms may be added to the basic form.

MONOFOLD MASKS   Masks can also be constructed by using the monofold technique. Since our faces are symmetrical, the monofold technique can be used to achieve a symmetrical pattern. The fold of the paper runs vertically, and sections such as the eyes, mouth and nose may be cut from both thicknesses of the folded sheet. Figure 66 shows the addition of paper horns or ears and a beard to the basic form. Two brass paper fasteners and a rubber band might be added to hold the mask to the face.

PAPER BAG MASKS   The paper bag offers a ready-made cube which can be built upon and decorated as a mask. Children should place the bag over their heads so as to locate the position of the eyes and mouth. After these areas are marked, the mask is removed and these features are cut away. In Figure 67, David (C.A. 15.8, I.Q. 70) has painted his mask with tempera. Scrap materials and additional paper-sculpture forms might have been added.

CYLINDRICAL FORMS   The process for constructing cylinders, previously described, can lead to some interesting forms. Narrow and wide stripes of paper should be provided so that children can curl the strips into cylinders and combine them in a variety of ways. Figure 68 illustrates how a rabbit might be constructed. Three cylinders are joined together to form the head and body, and ears are added. In Figure 69, a low, crawling animal is constructed from a number of combined paper cylinders.

FLOWERS   For constructing flowers, the cone shape is most frequently used. Figure 70 shows one method for constructing a blossom from paper. A circle is made, and a slit is cut from the edge of the circle to the exact center. Sections are removed along the edge of the circle to create petals. The edges of the slit are overlapped and glued to form the cone. The point of the cone is flattened against a background sheet of paper and glued in place.

Figure 67 (left). A paper bag provides a cube which lends itself to the consruction of a mask. By David (C. A. 15.8, I. Q. 70).

Figure 68 (right). Paper strips, shaped into cylinders, may be joined to form animals, people, etc. A rabbit is pictured here.

Figure 69 (left, below). Paper cylinders are united to create a low, crawling animal (a dachshund, perhaps).

Figure 70 (right, below). A paper circle, with a slit cut from the edge to the center, provides one method for constructing a flower blossom.

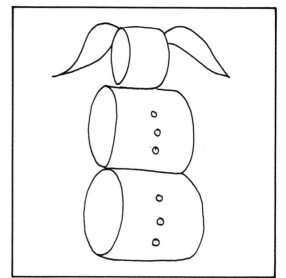

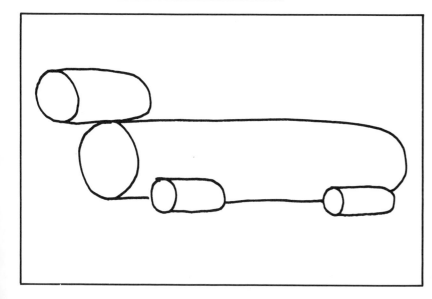

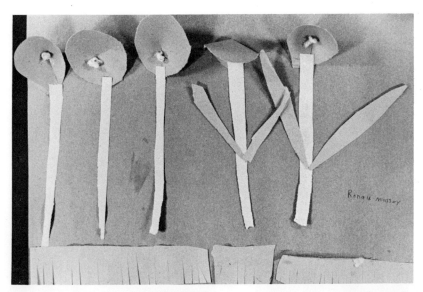

In Figure 71 Ronald (C.A. 11, I.Q. 67) has created a garden of flowers by using the cone form. Karen (C.A. 13.5, I.Q. 50) has cut slits along the edges of her central flower to suggest petals in Figure 72. Scott (C.A. 11.7, I.Q. 71) has placed two cones, one within the other, to construct his blossoms in Figure 73.

Figure 71 (left, above). Ronald (C. A. 11, I. Q. 67) has constructed a garden full of flowers by using the cone shape.

Figure 72 (left, below). Karen (C. A. 13.5, I. Q. 50) has slit the edges of one of her blossoms to suggest petals.

Figure 73 (below). Scott (C. A. 11.7, I. Q. 71) has used cones within cones to create multi-colored blossoms.

HATS   Working with paper strips, invite children to see how many different ways a hat might be constructed. Mike (C.A. 10.9, I.Q. 76) has stapled a few strips together to create a band which fits over the crown of the head. Another band, shaped like a feather, is attached to the band, thereby creating an Indian hat (Figure 74).

Bobby (C.A. 13.6, I.Q. 64) has covered the crown band with many long strips which are stapled to the band and cross to the other side to be attached to the opposite side of the crown band (Figure 75).

Terry (C.A. 12.9, I.Q. 80) has also covered his crown band with a few paper strips which have opposite ends attached to the band. A couple of paper strip streamers are attached, one displaying colorful flowers (Figure 76).

Mike (C.A. 10.9, I.Q. 76) was not attracted by the idea of constructing a hat and decided, instead, to create a paper sculptured shoe, as seen in Figure 77. He cut a number of slits in a sheet of paper and curled up the sides to make the three-dimensional shoe. A paper band runs across the top of the shoe. Retarded children often digress from a suggested art topic, and these digressions should be accepted. The personal interests of children should be given priority if the art activity is to be meaningful to them.

Figure 74 (above). Paper strips may be assembled in a number of ways to create a hat. A paper feather is attached to this Indian hat by Mike (C. A. 10.9, I. Q. 76).

Figure 75 (right). Paper strips cover the dome of the hat created by Bobby (C. A. 13.6, I. Q. 64).

Figure 77 (right).   Mike (C. A. 10.9, I. Q. 76) decided to create a shoe from his sheets of construction paper.   Retarded children often digress from a selected art topic.

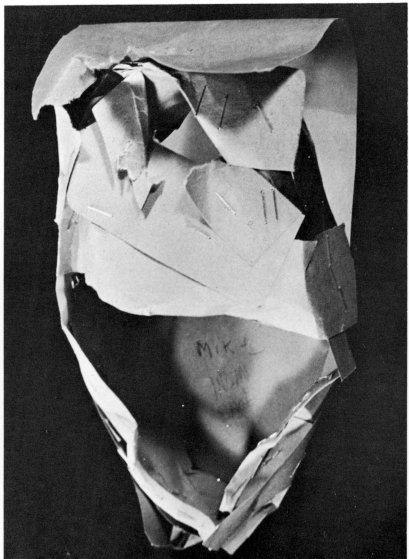

Figure 76 (below).   Flowers are attached to the streamers of this hat by Terry (C. A. 12.9, I. Q. 80).

PAPER PLATE FIGURES   The paper plate may provide an interesting approach to paper sculpture. Plates may be cut into strips, folded or shaped into a cone. Two plates may be joined by cutting slits halfway through each plate. In Figure 78 Dawn (C.A. 8, M.A. 7) has constructed a person by attaching a number of cut and whole plates together with brass paper fasteners. Crayons were used to provide detail.

Figure 78. Paper plates have been cut, folded, formed and assembled to create this figure by Dawn (C. A. 8, M. A. 7).

Mosaics

The mosaic technique can provide rewarding experiences for the retarded, provided the background space to be covered is not too large and the tesserae are large in size so that the job does not become tedious.

To motivate the retarded, show them illustrations of the resplendent mosaics that flourished to great heights during the ninth century. Explain that a mosaic is a design executed in small pieces of stone or colored glass, called tesserae, set in cement.

Preliminary designs for a mosaic should be kept very simple because the materials (tesserae) will add much detail and busyness to the composition.

Various types of paper may be used to create a mosaic. Dissimilar shapes may be cut with a scissors or torn into bits. Various seeds, used as tesserae, provide rich contrasts in color, texture and size. A visit to a pet or aquarium shop will provide numerous sources. Rice and corn may be soaked in food coloring or cold water dye to create light and dark colors. Watermelon seeds, split peas, beans, oats, barley, wheat, red Indian corn, yellow field corn and white popcorn may all find their way into a mosaic. Eggshells, used in their natural color or dyed in food coloring, make excellent tesserae. Other materials, such as pebbles, buttons, macaroni (painted with tempera) and sea shells may also be glued to a background of cardboard, tagboard, Masonite, plywood or other substantial materials to create a mosaic. Elmer's glue provides an excellent adhesive.

In Figures 79 and 80 two companion pieces were created by Evelyn (C.A. 47). Black nylon cord was first glued to cardboard to establish the outline of the flower forms. Next, aquarium gravel was used in a variety of colors for the tesserae.

Stitchery

Stitchery is one art technique which the retarded thoroughly enjoy once they understand a few of the techniques.

MATERIALS   For beginners, natural burlap provides one of the most suitable background materials for stitchery. Natural burlap may be obtained most inexpensively from an upholstery shop.   Other materials on which stitchery might be executed include percale, muslin, linen, buckram, burlap feed bags, vegetable bags, crinoline and monk's cloth.   I have seen some perfectly lovely stitchery executed on screen, normally used for screen doors and windows.   An old window screen, if clean and free of rust, provides an interesting background upon which to work.   And the screen is already framed, making it easy to work with.   Screen will not pucker if students pull their thread too tightly—a problem often encountered with burlap if the necessary instructions have not been given.

A tapestry needle, number 13 or 14, is an excellent tool for stitching yarns and threads into burlap.   A tapestry needle has a large eye, making it easy to thread, and a blunt point which is safe to handle.

Stitchery projects are especially beautiful when a variety of yarns and threads are used.   Search for cotton or wool yarns of various weights and textures.   Needlepoint yarns, 4-ply knitting yarn, rug filler, carpet warp, string, embroidery floss, crochet cotton, darning cotton and raffia may all be applied to burlap.

Colored pieces of felt and patterned pieces of cloth may be appliqued to the burlap.   For variety in texture, use velvet, gingham, flannel, leather, corduroy and silks.

Beads, buttons, sequins and metallic yarns provide interesting contrasts in texture.

STITCHES   Figures 81 through 83 show a number of stitches which may be introduced to the retarded.   The hooking stitch, not pictured, is made by drawing the thread through the burlap, forming loops which extend above the surface of the burlap (the pile).

When first introducing stitchery to the retarded, the teacher should not overwhelm students by introducing a wide variety of stitches.   During the first experience, it might be wise to demonstrate only the running stitch and the chain stitch, the most popular in children's designs. Later, as experience is gained, additional stitches may be introduced. Figures 84 through 86 show retarded children's first experiences with stitchery.

DEVELOPING DESIGNS   From the standpoint of design, all three examples fail in certain ways.   Shapes lack unity and are not united.   Most of the designs are restricted to a simple line design and lack rich areas of texture and pattern.   Teachers of the retarded must learn to accept the honest endeavors of their students.   The learning experience and the avenue of expression are of greater importance than the creation of beautiful art objects.

Figures 79 and 80.   The mosaic technique can be employed by the retarded if the tesserae are large and the background to be covered is small.   In these two companion pieces Evelyn (C. A. 47) has glued nylon cord and colored aquarium gravel, serving as the tesserae, onto cardboard.

In beginning a stitchery project, students might be encouraged to create a scribble design. Using a long piece of rug filler, the yarn might be overlapped upon the surface of the burlap so as to create shapes of various sizes. Straight pins may be used to hold the scribble design in place until it is permanently stitched upon the burlap. Next, using the various stitches, the student is ready to fill some of the designated shapes with patterns. Some shapes may be left plain for the sake of contrast.

Some students may prefer cutting designs from newspaper. When interesting shapes are achieved, trace around the pattern with crayon and begin to sew.

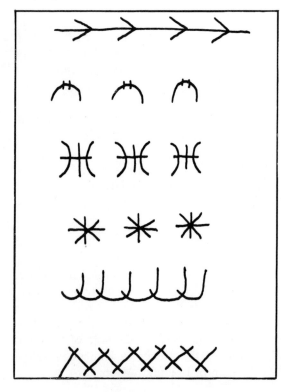

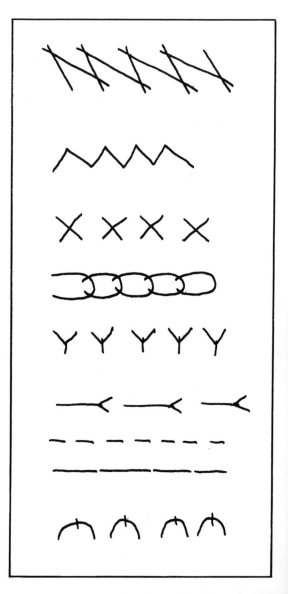

Figures 81 and 82. Pictured are some of the stitches which may be applied to burlap. Figure 81 (left), top to bottom: Fern Stitch, Lazy Daisy Tied Twice, Bundle Stitch, Double Cross Stitch, Blanket Stitch, Catch Stitch; Figure 82 (right), top to bottom: Feather Stitch, Zig-Zag Running Stitch, Cross Stitch, Chain Stitch, Short Y Stitch, Long Y Stitch, Running Stitch, Closed Running Stitch, Lazy Daisy Stitch.

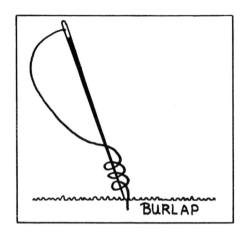

Figure 83. For the French knot, yarn is wound once, twice, and sometimes three times around the tapestry needle.

Figure 84 (left, below). Steve (C. A. 16.4, I. Q. 77) has used both the running stitch and the blanket stitch in his product.

Figure 85 (right). Kim (C. A. 15.1, I. Q. 70) was content to use the running stitch throughout her composition.

Figure 86 (right, below). Sue (C. A. 15.1, I. Q. 70) has used the running stitch to create various scattered shapes.

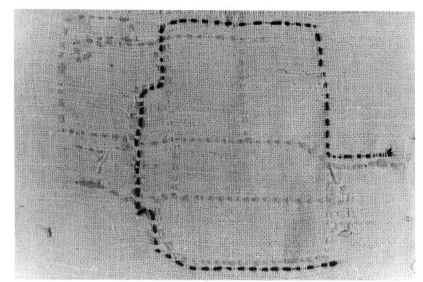

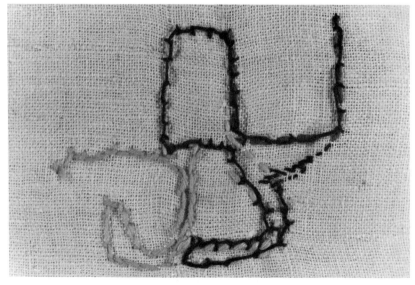

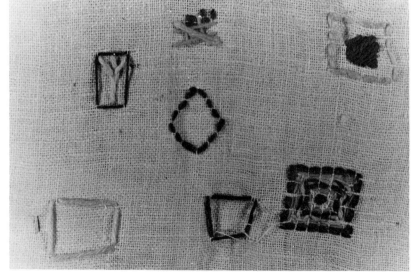

Puppetry

VALUES   In considering art materials and techniques for the retarded, puppetry must certainly rate high on the list. The creation and manipulation of puppets offers many rewards. Through puppetry, teachers are given an excellent opportunity to observe the retarded in play and conversation. As children speak for their inanimate creatures, teachers are able to "tune in" to the frustrations, joys and emotional feelings of the puppeteers.

The retarded often experience a delay in speech development and are sometimes discouraged by their inability to express themselves effectively. But when speaking for a puppet, the child loses his inhibitions as thoughts and ideas are extended from the self to the puppet. Courage is found in speaking for another. Even quiet, withdrawn children effectively lose their inhibitions when speaking before their classmates.

Puppetry is a social activity. Children learn that they are dependent upon each other in achieving success. There must be interaction for the sake of the show. Children view others in a new light. They realize that together they can create something quite wonderful which cannot be done alone. Increased intimacy and friendship between students and teacher develop as the pleasurable aspects of puppetry are enjoyed.

The variety of talents called upon means that all students are active. Artists are needed to create the puppets. Sometimes a backdrop must be painted or drawn. Some children are stagehands, others serve as actors, costumers, playwrights.

MOTIVATION   Occasionally, the retarded find difficulty in creating dialogue for their puppets once they are created. The teacher may need to set the imaginations of children in action by telling a story which the children are able to enlarge upon.

A simple story, filled with action, might be needed: "John had a habit of playing ball near the home of his neighbor. John's mother warned him to stay away from the neighbor's windows. But as John threw the ball, he forgot his mother's warnings, and crept farther and farther onto his neighbor's lawn. Suddenly, John threw the ball especially hard, and guess what happened? There was a large crash! The ball flew right through the neighbor's large picture window. Out came John's neighbor. What do you think John's mother said to him? What do you think the neighbor had to say?"

Figures 87 and 88. Left, in constructing a paper bag puppet, the mouth may be made to speak by pasting or drawing the top lip on the bottom flap of the upside-down bag, and the bottom lip on the side of the bag. The hand, inserted into the bag, synchronizes lip movements with speech. Right, fluttering eyes may be made by attaching eyelids to the bottom flap of an upside-down paper bag. The eyes are located on the side of the bag.

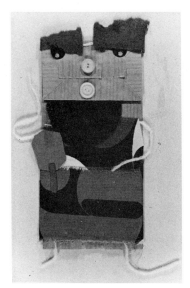

Figure 89. Felt, buttons, construction paper, pipe cleaners and cloth were glued to a paper bag to form this puppet by Karen (C. A. 13.5, I. Q. 50).

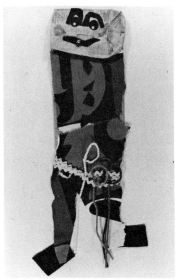

Figure 90. Long legs adorn this puppet. The hanging pipe cleaners represent pipes, one of which is to be used daily for smoking. By Terry (C. A. 12.9, I. Q. 80).

METHODS: *Paper Bag Puppets*   The paper bag provides a basic shape for creating a simple puppet. The bag can be used in two basic ways to create the head. (1) The bottom flap of the upside-down bag can be the top lip, while the bottom lip is on the side of the bag (Figure 87). With the hand and fingers inside the bag, the flap can be manipulated in such a way as to synchronize lip movements with the spoken word. (2) The bottom flap can contain the eye lids (rather than the lips) while the eyes themselves are found on the side of the bag (Figure 88). If positioned correctly, the eyes open and close when the flap is raised and lowered. With this method the mouth is located farther down the side of the bag and cannot be manipulated.

A body is easily attached: additional paper bags can be stuffed to serve as body, arms and legs and added to the paper bag head with brass paper fasteners. Examples of paper bag puppets are seen in Figures 89 and 90.

Stick Puppets   Stick puppets are also simple to construct. A long stick forms the backbone of the puppet. A piece of nylon hose may be placed over a cotton ball to form the head. A rubber band will hold the gathered nylon to the stick, which is inserted up into the head. Newspaper rolled into a tube may be held to the stick with rubber bands and bent to form the legs and hands. This basic framework may then be dressed with cloth and other bits of scrap materials (Figure 91).

The process of making a stick puppet may be simplified to a greater degree. A two-dimensional figure may be cut from paper and pasted to a stick. The stick may be controlled behind the edge of a table top as children make the puppet perform (Figure 92).

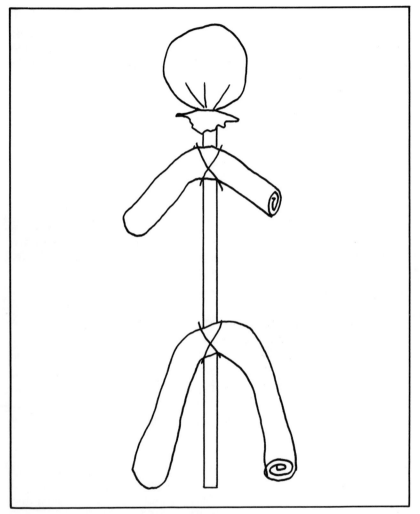

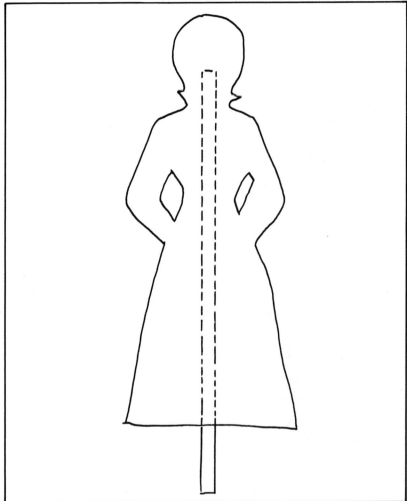

Figure 91.   Nylon, cotton batting and newspaper tubes are attached to a stick to create the frame for the stick puppet.   Paper or cloth may be used to clothe the puppet.

Figure 92.   A two-dimensional figure may be cut from paper and pasted to a stick to create a simple stick puppet.

Sock Puppets   A cotton stocking provides the foundation for the sock puppet.   The sock is placed over the hand, with cloth indented between the thumb and forefinger to form the mouth.   Pieces of colored cloth can be glued or sewn over the indenture to suggest the mouth or tongue.   A piece of folded cardboard inserted into the sock will better define the top and lower sections of the mouth, which is controlled by the thumb and forefinger.

A variety of materials may be attached to suggest hair.   Strands of yarn, for example, could be gathered and sewn onto the top of the puppet's head, near the heel.   Buttons, sequins, buckles and other materials might suggest the eyes.   Felt, buttons, cork and other materials could be attached for the nose (Figure 93).

Fruit and Vegetable Puppets   Fruit and vegetable puppets might well serve as an introduction to puppetry.   A clothespin, Tinkertoy stick, tongue depressor or lollipop stick is inserted into a head made from a potato, apple or orange.   Bits of cloth, buttons, jewelry, ribbon, ric-rac and other scrap materials may be added for clothing and decorative accessories.

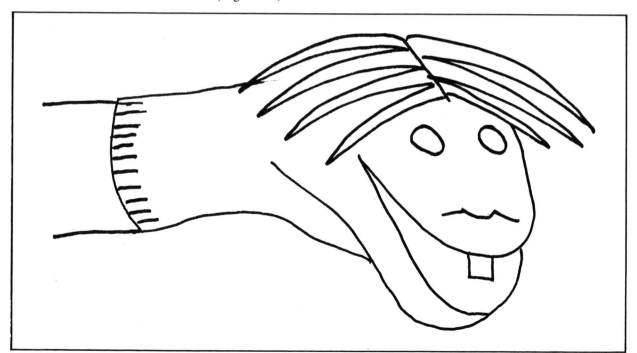

Figure 93. A woolen sock, decorated with scrap materials, makes an excellent puppet.

Clay

PINCH POT METHOD   The pinch pot methods might well serve as an introduction to clay, as the technique is simple and the results are gratifying.   Clay is rolled into a ball and held in the palm of one hand.   The thumb of the other hand is pressed into the ball of clay as the ball is turned in the palm of the hand. The walls of the pinch pot become thinner and thinner as the thumb presses the rotating pot against the palm of the hand.   A pencil eraser, tongue depressor, nail head and other tools may be used to press an interesting texture onto the sides of the pinch pot.   When dry, the clay pot can be fired and glazed (Figure 94).

PILE METHOD   To construct a pot by means of the pile method, a base for the pot must first be made.   Flatten a ball of clay into a circle, making certain the "pancake" is of even thickness.   Next, roll little balls of clay and place them along the outer edge of the "pancake" base.   Build up the balls of clay as a bricklayer would lay bricks.   Press and pinch the balls together so that all holes are eliminated and the walls of the vase are smooth and of even thickness (Figure 95).

COIL METHOD   When constructing a coil pot, the base of the vase is fashioned in the manner just described for the pile method.   In building up the sides of the base, long coils of clay are encircled around the base and built up, one upon the other, until the desired height is reached.   Coils are made by rolling out pieces of clay, using the palm of the hand, into long "snakes."   The coils are later pinched together, smoothed out and blended so that the coils are no longer visible (Figure 96).

SLAB METHOD   To create objects with the slab method, clay must be rolled out into thick sheets.   A piecrust roller and two wooden sticks, identical in thickness and placed on either side of the clay, enable the ceramist to roll out sheets of clay which are of even thickness (Figure 97).   The slabs of clay are cut and joined to create a variety of objects.   Figure 98 illustrates how a rectangular box might appear.   Areas to be joined are roughened with a tool or knife.   Slip (clay thinned with water) is applied to the roughened areas before they are joined.

ANIMALS   Demonstrate how balls and cylinders can be molded from clay by using the palms and fingertips.   Join cylinders of varying size together to form the bodies and legs, necks and arms of people and animals.   Apply slip to roughened ends when joining sections together.   Also try to pull out the features of animals and people from a single piece of clay, thus eliminating the need to join separate pieces together.   When dry, fire and glaze the ceramic pieces.

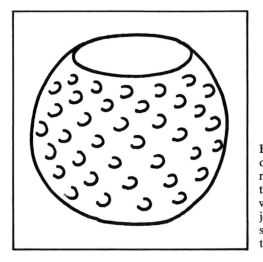

Figure 94. The thumb of one hand is pressed into a rotating ball of clay held in the other hand to thin the walls of the pinch pot. Objects may be pressed into the sides of the pinch pot to add texture.

Figure 95. Balls of clay are built up upon a "pancake" base in the pile method.

Figure 96. Clay is rolled into snakes or coils and built up upon a base for the coil method.

Figure 98 (right). The slabs may be joined together to create a variety of objects having walls of even thickness.

Figure 97 (below, right). Two sticks on either side of the clay and a piecrust roller enable the ceramist to create slabs of clay which are of even thickness.

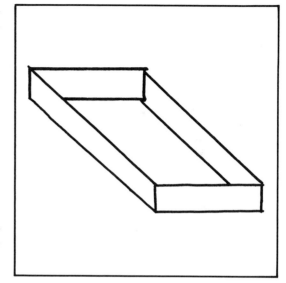

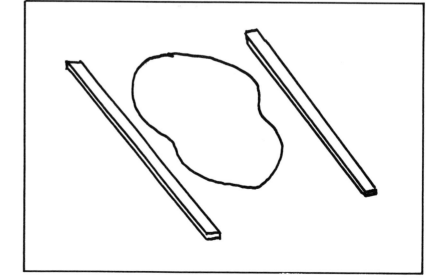

Finger Painting

Finger paints may be introduced when the retarded are able to use this material in an artistic way. If children are enraptured with the sticky, pastelike consistency of finger paint, the material should be withheld until the child shows evidence that he is ready to manipulate the material in an artistic manner.

RECIPES: *Flour and Water*   Mix flour and salt with water to form a paste; add food coloring. Spread on commercial finger paint paper or a glazed shelf paper.

Shaving Soap   Squirt nonmentholated shaving soap directly onto a Formica or porcelain table top; sprinkle powdered tempera from a large salt shaker into the soap. Add water when the soap dries. Wipe the table top when finished.

Liquid Starch   Apply one tablespoon of liquid starch (Sta-Flo) or more to the finger paint paper; shake powdered tempera into the starch for coloring; add water if necessary.

Crayon Techniques

SCRIBBLING STAGE   When the retarded are scribblers and do not yet reveal representational symbols in their art work, large black crayons and large sheets of smooth paper encourage free movement of the hand and arms.

CRAYON RESIST   The crayon resist technique is a great favorite of the retarded. Two color approaches are used. In method one, light colored crayons are heavily applied to a light colored paper, and a dark wash of tempera paint is painted over the light crayon colors. Figure 99 by Steve (C.A. 16.4, I.Q. 77) illustrates how the bright crayon colors, consisting of wax, resist the black tempera wash.

In method two, dark colored crayons are applied heavily to sheets of dark colored construction paper. Next, a light colored tempera wash is applied. The light wash may consist of white tempera, thinned with water; or a tinted wash (a drop of red added to the white to create pink, for example) may be used.

In using both techniques, children should be cautioned to press their crayons heavily upon paper so that enough wax is deposited to effectively resist the added wash.

CRAYON STENCIL   The crayon stencil technique successfully introduces the retarded to the principle of repetition in design. A shape (stencil) is cut or torn from paper. Wax crayon or pastel is smeared along the edges of the paper stencil. Next, the crayoned stencil is placed on a sheet of colorful background paper. Using radiating movements, the crayon is smeared from the edges of the stencil onto the background paper. The stencil is next recrayoned and the smearing process is repeated. In Figure 100, the crayon was applied directly to the stencil and the background paper in one simple operation, thereby creating a repeat design consisting of an apple motif. In Figure 101 the crayon was traced around the stencil, directly upon the background paper, to create the repeated shapes, which were later shaded in with crayon. A variety of approaches become evident as exploration is encouraged.

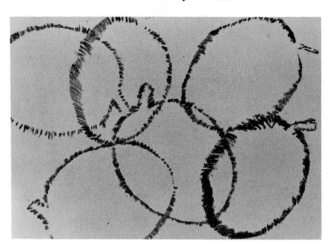

Figure 99. Light colored crayon was heavily applied to manila paper, then painted over with a black wash of tempera paint to create this crayon resist drawing by Steve (C. A. 16.4, I. Q. 77).

Figure 100. Crayon was rubbed directly from a cut stencil onto the background paper to create this stenciled repeat design.

Figure 101. Crayon was traced around a cut paper stencil to create this repeated design. The traced shapes were shaded in with crayon.

Figures 102 to 104 (above and facing page).   Duplicated name designs by retarded students.   Note that Anna (Figure 103) has created a gay figure based on her duplicated name.

DUPLICATED NAME DESIGNS   Fold a sheet of paper so that a central crease runs parallel with the two longest sides of the paper.   Using crayon write your name or that of a friend on the fold.   Press hard so that the lines are indented upon the other half of the folded sheet.   Open the sheet and, using crayon, follow the impression on the other half of the folded sheet, thereby creating a mirror image of the name.   Next embellish the letters and background spaces with solid shapes and patterns, using crayon.   Figures 102, 103 and 104, by retarded students, reveal the interesting results which may be obtained with this technique.

ENCAUSTIC   Crayons may also be used as a painting medium, when melted.   Commercial hot pallettes are available which safely melt crayons into a liquid.   Using a stiff bristle brush, tongue depressor, lollipop stick or pallette knife, the melted crayons are applied to a background of paper, cardboard, Masonite or canvas.   A Q-tip, from the drug store, provides an excellent tool for applying dots of color upon paper—suggesting the technique, pointillism, for which Seurat was famous.

BACKGROUND MATERIALS   Unusual background materials may be sought to instill a renewed interest in an old tool—the crayon.   Encourage children to experiment with the use of crayon on cloth or on paper bags which have been crushed in water and dried to simulate leather.   Experiment by laying out interesting designs on the want-ad sections of the newspaper or on graph paper.   Use crayon on sandpaper, and create a transfer design by applying a heated flat iron to newsprint positioned over the crayon-on-sandpaper design.

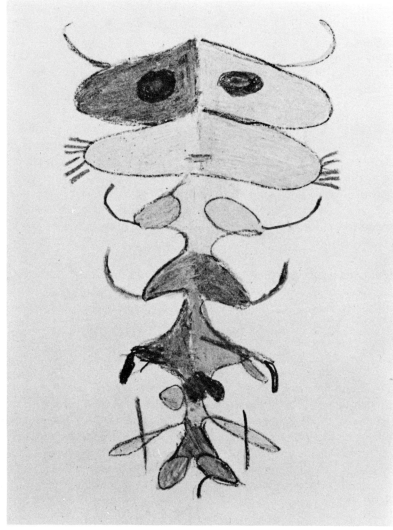

CRAYON RELIEF   Experiment with various textured materials. Place mesh vegetable bags, cut cardboard shapes, plastic doilies, netting and other materials beneath thin newsprint and rub the newsprint with the peeled side of a crayon to pick up the texture of the materials below. Cut interesting shapes from the textured pieces and construct a collage.

CRAYON ETCHING   The crayon etching technique may be explored by the more competent retarded students. Paper, such as tagboard, manila or white drawing paper, is solidly covered with a single crayon color or juxtaposed shapes of solid crayon color. India ink is painted over the solid wax layer and allowed to dry. A sharp tool, such as a pencil point, nail point or ice pick, is used to etch a design into the black ink, revealing the warm light crayon colors below.

Black tempera containing a tablespoon of liquid or powdered detergent may be used as a substitute for the India ink. Black crayon and certain brands of dark shoe polish may likewise serve as an effective substitute.

Collage Techniques

The term "papiers colles," indicating glued papers, comes from the French language and refers to a method which involves the pasting of paper pieces, newspaper, various textured materials and illustrations to a heavy background such as chipboard. The collage technique was an outgrowth of the French Cubist movement, and was practiced by such artists as Georges Braque, Max Ernst, Pablo Picasso and Jean Arp. These artists frequently emphasized both texture and line when rendering their collages.

As practiced today, in schools, a wide variety of materials commonly find their way into a collage. Scrap materials, including bits of cloth, paper, netting, and unusual materials such as metallic foil, theatre tickets, gum wrappers, etc., may be used in a collage. A rich supply of scrap materials, Elmer's glue and a sturdy background material are all that is needed to stir interest in the collage technique.

The collages pictured in Figures 105 through 109 were created by retarded students from construction paper of assorted colors. Students were encouraged to cut shapes which varied in size so as to avoid monotony in repetition. Also, students were invited to cut shapes which seemed to correlate well. "Perhaps all of your shapes should have curved edges, or straight edges, or zigzagged edges. See if you can cut shapes with edges which are somewhat alike when pasted on background paper."

Figures 105 to 109 (facing page). Construction paper was used to create the collages pictured here. Students were encouraged to vary the size of their repeated shapes and to cut edges which correlated properly within the composition.

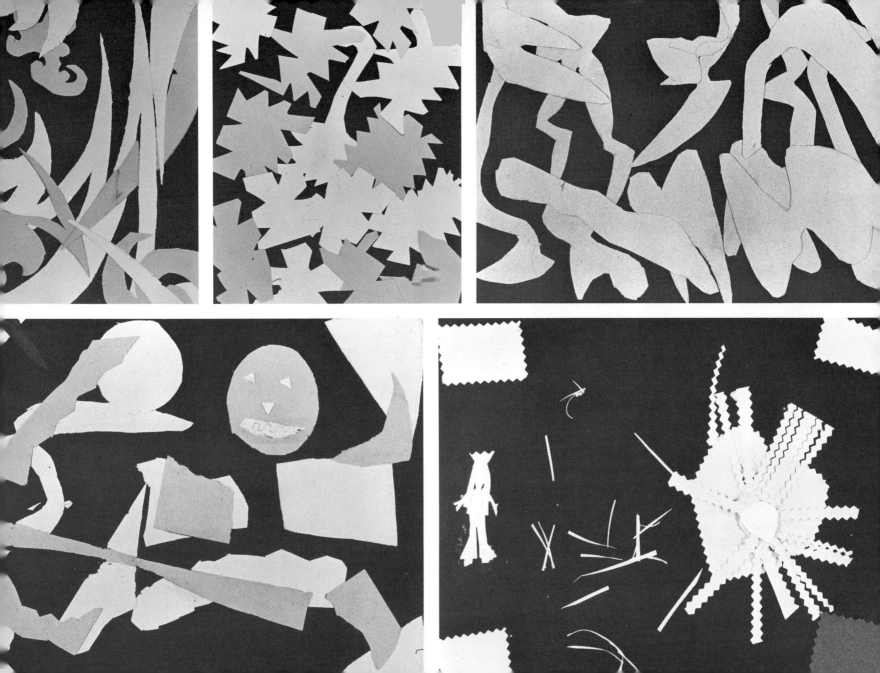

Woodworking

MATERIALS   As an introduction to woodworking, scrap pieces of lumber, a hammer and nails will serve the needs and interests of the retarded.   Often lumber yards will donate scrap pieces of lumber when informed of its use.   Small pieces, varying in size and shape, should be selected.   White pine and poplar are especially suitable as they are soft woods, making it easy to pound nails so as to join pieces.   Encourage the construction of animals and people as well as free forms.   Shoe polish in various colors provides an excellent stain.

As children mature and their hand-eye coordination improves, introduce them to a variety of tools for working with wood.   Appropriate tools would include:

Hammer
Nails, various sizes
Hack saw, miter saw, coping saw, crosscut saw
Screwdriver
Square
File
Wood clamps, including the C clamp
Chisel
Pliers
Wrench
Plane
Sandpaper

Demonstrate the uses for each tool, and stress safety measures in using the tools.   Label the tools so that children can identify them, and paint a silhouette of the tool on the wall so that children are easily able to return the tools to their appropriate places.

Older children will enjoy using soft woods such as white pine, Douglas fir and bass plywoods in various thicknesses.   Woods may be finished with a variety of materials, including crayon rubbed with turpentine, wood stains, shellac, lacquer, varnish and enamel.

PROJECTS   Children enjoy constructing articles which are functional.   Items such as pencil holders, tie racks, breadboards, hot pads, letter holders, stepbenches, bookends, magazine racks, bird houses, bookcases, baskets and napkin holders may be constructed from wood.   Encourage children, as much as possible, to use their own ideas in designing and decorating their articles.   Avoid patterns and how-to-do-it instructions which might replace a creative experience.

Weaving

Weaving techniques afford creative and rewarding art avenues for the retarded.   Many weaving processes are simple yet produce patterns which are aesthetically pleasing.

PAPER WEAVING   When weaving with paper, a sheet of colored construction paper becomes a *loom*, i.e., the instrument upon which to weave.   Often the sheet is folded once so that slits may be cut perpendicular to the fold, terminating one inch or "two fingers" away from the two edges opposite the fold.   The slits correspond with the *warp*, the vertical strands which are threaded upon the loom.   Paper strips correspond with the *woof*, the horizontal strands which are woven in and out of the warp.

When weaving with paper a checkerboard pattern can hardly be avoided if strips, even in width, are woven in and out, out and in, in and out of the slits (see Figure 110).   To avoid the monotony of shapes visible in the checkerboard pattern, encourage children to vary the spacings between the cut slits (Figure 111).   Second, encourage children to weave with paper strips which vary in width.   And third, the monotonous shapes of the checkerboard pattern may be avoided if slits are skipped occasionally during the weaving process. Weave, horizontally, over two slits, under three slits, over one slit, etc.

For the sake of greater variety, encourage children to cut slits (warp) into their folded paper which are not always perpendicular to the fold of the paper (Figure 112). Try combining straight, perpendicular slits with curved and angular slits as illustrated in Figure 113, to achieve interesting results.

Designs are usually symmetrical when the paper loom is folded during the cutting process. To create asymmetrical designs, try cutting slits into a paper loom which has not been folded, as illustrated in Figure 114. Figure 115 illustrates a finished product: curved slits were cut into a non-folded paper loom and paper strips of varying widths were woven in and out of the curved slits.

Figure 110. When weaving paper, in and out movements often result in a checkerboard having monotonous, repetitious shapes.

Figure 111. When the spacing between slits cut into the folded paper loom is varied, the monotony of a checkerboard pattern is eliminated.

Figure 112. Try cutting diagonal or slanting slits into a paper loom to achieve unusual results.

Figure 113. Slits may be perpendicular to the fold, curved and angular.

Figure 114. Slits cut into a paper loom which has not been folded result in an asymmetrical design.

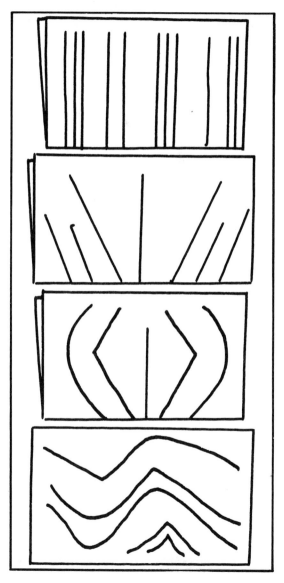

Figure 115.   In this example strips of paper, varying in width, were woven into curved slits cut into a non-folded paper loom.

CARDBOARD LOOM WEAVING   Cardboard, used in place of paper, may also provide a suitable loom upon which to weave.   Evenly spaced notches are cut along opposite edges of the loom.   Yarn, string, cord, raffia or thread, serving as warp, is inserted into notch 1 (see Figure 116), next run across the loom into notch 2, forward into notch 3, across the front of the loom into notch 4, etc.

It is possible to weave on both sides of the cardboard loom if both sides of the loom are threaded.   Yarn may be inserted into notch 1, across the front of the loom into notch 2, across the opposite side and down into notch 4, across the front of the loom into notch 3, across the back of the loom into notch 5, etc.   After threading, such woof materials as yarn, ribbon and cord are woven in and out of the warp.

FRAME LOOM WEAVING   In frame loom weaving, an old picture frame might serve as the loom, or four pieces of lumber nailed together as seen in Figure 117 would provide an excellent loom.   Nails, evenly spaced, are driven along opposite sides of the loom to hold the warp.

CARTON LOOM WEAVING   In carton loom weaving, milk cartons, ice cream cartons, oatmeal cartons and other cartons of various sizes and shapes serve as the loom.   In Figure 118 long, narrow paper strips, evenly spaced, run along the sides of the loom.   Opposite ends of the strips are glued along the upper, inside rim of the carton and along the bottom of the carton.   Horizontal paper strips are then woven into the vertical warp.

In Figure 119 evenly spaced notches were cut along the top rim of the carton loom.   To thread the warp, yarn or string is inserted into notch 1.   The yarn is run down the side of the carton, across the bottom and

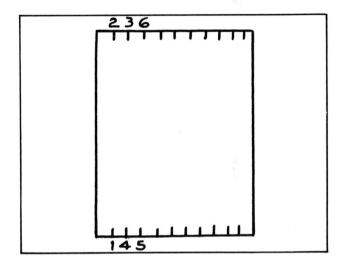

Figure 116.   A sheet of cardboard can serve as a loom. Yarn is threaded into the notches as described in the text.

Figure 117.   An old picture frame or wooden frame serves as a loom.   Yarn warp is threaded on evenly spaced nails.

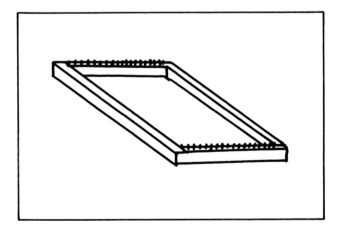

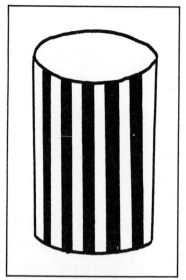

Figure 118. Vertical paper strips, glued directly to the carton along the inner top rim and bottom side, are the warp in this loom.

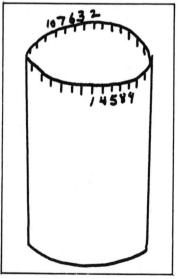

Figure 119. Alternatively, yarn threaded into evenly spaced notches cut along the top rim of the carton may serve as the warp.

up the opposite side into notch 2. Next the yarn is inserted into the neighboring notch 3. The yarn runs down the side of the loom, across the bottom (*crossing* the first strand positioned across the bottom of the loom) and up the front side of the loom, being secured in notch 4. The yarn is threaded in a counterclockwise direction as it fills the notches. After the carton is threaded, horizontal woof is next woven in and out of the vertical warp. The woven fabric always remains on the cardboard loom; it is not removed from the loom as in previously described methods.

KITTY LOOM WEAVING   Figure 120 illustrates how the kitty loom is constructed. Nails, evenly spaced, are driven around the central opening of the wooden loom. Figure 121 illustrates three ways in which the kitty loom can be threaded; the threading procedure moves from left to right. When the opposite end (right end) of the loom is reached, the yarn is threaded on the nails a second time, from right to left. And when the yarn is threaded over each nail the second time, the first yarn loop (located immediately below the second applied loop) is pulled over the head of the nail by means of a pick-up pin (a tool such as a nail or crochet hook) held in one hand. As each new loop is positioned on the nail, the previous loop lying below is pulled up and over the nail head. The weaving process runs from left to right, from right to left, from left to right, etc.

Figure 122 reveals the back side of the kitty loom and the woven product which emerges through the central opening. The woven fabric is a perfect tube when removed from the loom, much like the sleeve of a sweater. Slippers may be made by tying one end of the "sleeve" shut. Purses, marble bags, tennis shoe holders and other items may be made when one end of the "sleeve" is left open and the other end is sewed shut with yarn.

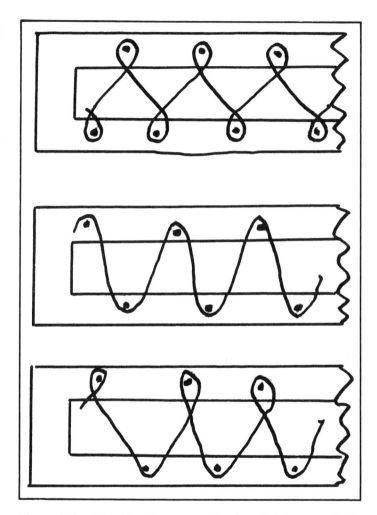

Figure 121. The kitty loom may be threaded in any of the three ways shown here.

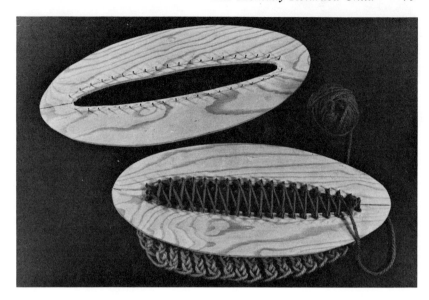

Figure 120. Pictured here is the kitty loom.

Figure 122. Pictured here is the reverse side of the kitty loom and the woven fabric which emerges through the central opening. Many useful articles may be woven upon the kitty loom.

The Blind Child

by Ruth Ancona

Art for the blind child differs from art for other children in degree, not in kind. To think of art as an activity that depends only on visual perception is to deprive the blind child of the enrichment and satisfaction of his own creativity.

Teaching art to the blind requires a great deal of individual attention. Is the child completely blind, or is he partially sighted? Has he always been blind, or does he have memories of visual perceptions? The child who is totally and congenitally blind has had less chance to form concrete images than the partially-sighted child or the child recently blinded, and each must be taught according to his perceptions of his world. The problem of the child's concrete perceptions is of major importance to his teacher. For example, the teacher may attempt to describe an orchid using every applicable adjective; but to hear of an orchid is not to actually see one, to touch or smell it. The art teacher must always be aware of each child's "idea" of an orchid, of his perception of the world around him.

TECHNIQUES

Many concepts and techniques take longer to explain and demonstrate to the blind child. However, this is balanced by the greater concentration and effort to understand that many of these children possess. For example, a blind child will spend several minutes positioning two pieces of paper to be stapled together until he is completely satisfied with the

effect. A spool marionette project further demonstrates the patience of blind children. Each child is given spools of assorted sizes. The spools are dipped into paint and then dried. Heavy-gauge twine is used to assemble the marionette: a length of it is threaded through the spools using a darning needle, bobby pin, or any other thin, pointed tool. The body and head are strung first, then the arms and legs. Each section is secured to prevent the spools from escaping, then attached to the body. The children enjoy linking the spools together, and rarely seem to lose patience when the spools fall off or the twine frays. Scrap materials (paper, felt, etc.) may be added to the marionette; once it is assembled, long threads are attached to the parts of the body which the child decides should be mobile. The child's concept of his own body, which is often weak in blind children, is strengthened as he examines the results of pulling one thread or another. Finally, the teacher may attach the strings to a cardboard square and the marionette can be made to perform his tricks.

It has sometimes been thought that the other senses of a blind person sharpen and improve to compensate for the loss of sight. However, the blind child's senses of hearing and touch do not always give him the same information that other children get through their sight. The teacher must be aware of what the child is perceiving, and must add the necessary corrections and explanations. Raised-line drawings, in which the paper is embossed with a relief image of a map or object, may present problems. The sighted child sees the entire overview, and then his eyes move to the small details. The blind child must depend on

his fingers, and perceives the drawing in small parts. Thus an overview is difficult for him to achieve, and criss-crossed lines, even if they are of different textures, may be misleading and frustrating. Raised-line drawings, then, should be used only in a limited way at first, and the teacher should make sure that each line is understood.

A recent innovation in teaching the blind is the Thermoform machine. Any object, up to about ½″ in height, is placed in the bed of the machine; through the action of intense heat, thin plastic sheets are vacuum-formed to a precisely detailed impression of the object. When the plastic sheet is removed, the shallow impression is filled with plaster, and the child has a model of his own which can be painted. Another tool is the screen board or tracing board, which can be constructed from a piece of plywood, approximately 18″ x 18″, covered with window screen. The child places his paper on top of the screen and then uses a stylus to trace around a cardboard pattern. The result is a very distinct raised line which is quite easy to follow with scissors. However, frequent use of materials of this sort, where the child has little or no direct control, will ultimately discourage his creativity. This is especially true when the model has been chosen or made by the teacher and the child's chance to exercise his imagination has been lost. The child himself is usually eager and anxious to test his skills and ideas, and the concepts he learns for himself are much more deeply ingrained.

Figure 123. A future teacher of the blind manipulates clay while wearing a blindfold. She is experiencing in a small way what it is like to create using only her tactile sense, and learning to identify with the creative needs of the handicapped child.

Sculpture is most often thought of as the basic medium of the blind, and indeed all children love to push and poke at clay. However, the introduction of the young blind child to clay must be carefully handled. Because his fingers tell him so much about his world, the blind child is not anxious to cover them with sticky paste, paint, clay or anything else that may impede his perception. Therefore, the teacher must reassure the child that the new material is not harmful and will indeed wash off. As the teacher manipulates the child's hands, he begins to understand the logistics of the medium; by his second experience, the child will have begun to make snakes, cars and other imaginative objects.

It is sometimes helpful to repeat a lesson, particularly with the young blind child. The first lesson is usually taken up with explaining the procedure and the materials, and the child is busy familiarizing himself with the processes involved. By the second lesson, the child has gained confidence and is ready to attack the problem before him. Basic skills, such as the making of paper chains or the folding of paper strips together to form a spring, should be returned to several times in the course of the year of art instruction. Of course, each time the end result may be varied so that the child does not lose interest. For example, for first and second graders, paper chains may be introduced at first as witches' skirts: black, orange and yellow rings are stapled together to form a waistband, and similar chains are then attached to the waistband to form the rest of the skirt. At Christmas, red and green chains make attractive room decorations; with the addition of paper berries and leaves, they become boughs of holly. Finally, in the spring, a green chain with pastel flowers attached becomes a daisy chain. Another example of a project which may be repeated throughout the year utilizes two strips of paper folded alternately together to form a spring. The young child often has difficulty in understanding the sequence of folding, and repetition is both helpful and necessary. A simple accordion snake is the easiest project to start with—large eyes are attached to one end of the spring, and the child has made an intricate, interesting object. Later on, the spring is used to make "Mr. Valentine." His body, head, hands and feet are valentine hearts, but his arms and legs are made from paper springs. When finished, "Mr. Valentine" can be made to dance and perform many astonishing feats, especially if his arms and legs are long and gangly. Invite the children to see how many different ways the paper chain or paper spring can be used—repetition of the technique does not mean that all children in the group will attain the same end result.

Many blind children enjoy using paints and crayons. Partially-sighted children are quite effective at utilizing color, and many children who have only light perception are able to tell dark colors from light and intense colors from pastels. Color can never be given second place in teaching art to these children, but must be stressed as an important part of the child's concept of the world.

A project which enables the children to cooperate in drawing and painting is the mural. Particularly when there are partially-sighted children in the group, murals turn out well and give the children the satisfaction of participating in a worth-while group effort. Roll-ends of newsprint, available free at most newspaper offices, make ideal paper for the mural. Group agreement on the subject of the mural is essential; the children may be guided to assign themselves appropriate tasks in completing the project, with the partially-sighted filling in the details after the blind children have outlined in broad strokes. Each child is occupied with his section of the whole and at the same time conscious of his neighbors' work. The teacher can assist the children's understanding of the whole by establishing a base line and calling attention to imbalances in the project. When it is completed, the children quite enjoy hanging the mural on the wall for the admiration of visitors and other children. Good subects for murals are those which contain many easily understood images and which leave room for everyday objects. For example, a Halloween mural can have myriad witches, ghosts and goblins, while leaving room for the boy whose passion is antique cars. Everyone, then, has a chance to express himself and contribute his own unique part to the whole.

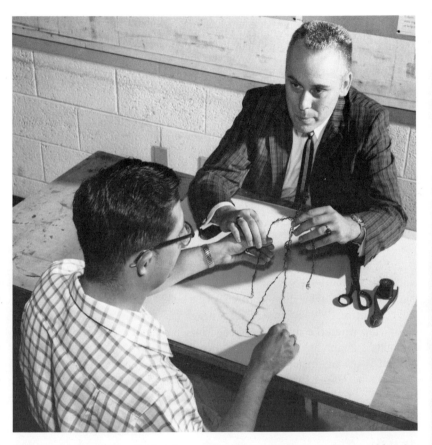

Figure 124 (above). As teacher and student run their hands over this wire sculpture figure, they are able to observe and discuss the student's art product.

Figure 125. The partially-sighted child's concept of a tree is seen in this painting of two fruit-tree blossoms with leaves. She views her environment at very close range and sees a small part of the object in a single glance. The teacher should encourage the blind child to observe subjects more closely and completely, so that separate views may be fused into a greater relation of the whole. Intense, brilliant and highly contrasting colors best suit the needs of the partially sighted.

Figure 126. "The Bicycle Rider" was created by a totally blind student. His familiarity with the object is revealed by the inclusion of many details: rumble seat, handlebars, pedals, etc. Although his handicap prevented him from steering a bicycle, the student had often ridden a bicycle built for two.

Even more than color, a complete understanding and appreciation of textures is essential to the blind child. Pasting or stapling materials of different textures aids the blind child in forming concepts and is enjoyable as well. A winter scene, for example, may be formed from wisps and tufts of cotton. Thin sheets of the kind of cotton used in packing jewelry may be cut or torn, then pasted on a dark-blue background for contrast; a snowstorm may be simulated with the tiny bits and pieces that are left over. When the scene is finished, each snowy area is easy for the blind or partially-sighted child to find. The younger child may be given a sack of such things as sandpaper, yarn, glitter, ribbon, junk jewelry, rug scraps, pieces of fur and burlap to be assembled on paper. Each texture seems to suggest the next, and the child becomes deeply involved in arranging and cutting the exact shapes needed for his assemblage. In the fall, the class can collect leaves that have fallen from trees, sorting them by shape and color, then pressing and drying them. Once dry, the leaves are sealed between two sheets of waxed paper with a warm iron. The child's ideas of the different uses of heat are expanded, and the texture of the leaves is perceptible through the layer of waxed paper. He learns about the art of composition as he arranges the leaves in a balanced and pleasing pattern on the paper.

For older children, the making of snowflakes by folding paper and then cutting or tearing out small areas may be a good textural experience. However, younger children find the idea of first folding the paper and then opening it out to discover the multiplied design a confusing one. The older child is better able to trace the steps involved and understand the process. Similarly, the Japanese art of origami (if the basic ideas taught can be applied creatively) is better used with older children. Instructions to "turn the paper this way, fold it that way" are confusing and frustrating to the younger child, especially the one who is totally blind.

Printing, too, can be used effectively in developing the blind child's sensitivity to texture. Simple block printing may be done with spools:

the end of the spool is dipped into paint, then pressed against soft, absorbent paper. The blind child can determine by touch which areas of the paper have been covered, and the partially-sighted child can construct ordered areas. For variety, clothespins, the ends of scrap blocks of wood, or other objects may be substituted for spools. Vegetable printing is a particularly useful technique, as it gives the children an understanding of the processes involved in reversing images. Christmas cards might be the basis for the project, with simple designs being carved into a potato, then printed with poster paint on construction paper. After instruction in the careful handling of the tools, older children are perfectly capable of incising their own designs.

Paper sculpture is especially useful when supplies are limited. The basic forms—cone, cylinder, cube and triangle—are carefully taught; the children can then assemble these forms to create a variety of objects. A Halloween mobile could be a project for a single child or for a group. Three paper rings, joined by thread with the largest at the bottom, form the basis of the mobile; various Halloween characters are attached to the rings, with the smallest ghost at the top and the largest pumpkin at the bottom. The mobile should be hung from the ceiling at child's-eye level, so that the smallest child will be able to examine all its parts at his leisure, noting the effects of breezes and air currents on the dancing witches. Rockets, space ships and flying saucers are always popular, and can be formed simply and satisfyingly from paper cones and cylinders. Once the children have mastered the basic techniques of paper sculpture through class projects of this sort, they should be encouraged to explore their own ideas.

Another very effective project involves the use of half-pint milk cartons, which may be assembled to create innumerable and varied animals, people and non-representational free forms. One approach to constructing a mouse might involve two large, round paper ears attached to the carton; a hole punched into the front of the carton and a paper cone inserted to form a long-pointed nose; beads attached with tape or straight pins for the eyes; and a long piece of yarn taped on for his tail.

For a pig, felt scraps could make pointed ears which flop forward; a paper cylinder might provide the nose; and curled paper (made by wrapping a thin strip of paper around a pencil), a tail.   An elephant may have huge paper ears and a paper-spring trunk.

A rewarding crafts project for younger children involves the weaving of paper strips into place mats.   Construction paper is folded lengthwise, and parallel cuts are made from the folded edge almost to the outside; various colored strips are woven in.

The making of hand puppets combines several media.   The central idea might be a circus, with each child choosing his favorite performer or animal.   The puppets' heads are formed from papier mache, hollowed out with a finger before they are totally dry; chicken wire may be used as a base for such hard-to-make details as an elephant's trunk.   Once dry, the heads can be painted and yarn hair, glitter, etc. may be added (if varnished, the heads will have a more durable finish).   The bodies are cloth, fastened by drawstrings around the puppets' necks.   These puppets may be the basis for the children's introduction to drama and the theater, or they may simply be toys—in any event, they provide opportunities for the children to use the techniques of sculpture and painting in creative, imaginative ways.

Art for the blind is an unlimited field.   Except in the rare cases where doctors advise otherwise, children should be encouraged to utilize what eyesight they have to the utmost.   The partially-sighted child can enjoy many media, and the blind child can learn to use even light perception to enhance his understanding and appreciation of the world.   Art for the blind should never be limited to the tactual—it differs in degree, not in kind, from the art of the seeing.

Afterword

Having briefly viewed the various types of exceptional children and their problems, one must agree that art experiences, creative in nature, can be of tremendous value in the general development of the exceptional child.   By experience and experimentation the teacher can provide the proper atmosphere for these values to be realized so that handicapped children may become adjusted, useful citizens of our society.

Bibliography

MISCELLANEOUS

Ahern, P. L. Art in special education at Luson. *School Arts*, May 1961, pp. 9-12.

Barlow, G. Creative education and the special student. *School Arts*, January 1964, p. 2.

Brenn, M. A. Arts and crafts in an educational program for handicapped children. *Exceptional Children*, May 1952, pp. 234-245.

Conant, H., & Randall, A. W. Special health problems. In *Art in education*. Peoria, Illinois: Charles A. Bennett, 1959, pp. 185-186.

Crawford, R. Art for exceptional children. *National Elementary Principal*, April 1951, pp. 25-29.

Hausman, J. J. Art, adjustment, and research. In *Art education for the exceptional child. Research Bulletin: Eastern Arts Association*. Kutztown, Pennsylvania: State Teachers College, 1956, pp. 21-23.

Helms, J. B. Art classes for aphasic children. *School Arts*, January 1964, pp. 35-36.

Koenig, F. G. Implications in the use of puppetry with handicapped children. *Exceptional Children*, January 1951, pp. 111, 112, 117.

Lowenfeld, V. The creative process and the handicapped. *School Arts*, March 1955, pp. 5-8.

Marksberry, M. L. Help them create. *Exceptional Children*, October 1957, pp. 80-83.

Neuber, M. A. What is the exceptional child? In *Art education for the exceptional child. Research Bulletin: Eastern Arts Association*. Kutztown, Pennsylvania: State Teachers College, 1956, pp. 5-7.

Randall, A. W. Art time for exceptional children. *School Arts*, April 1952, pp. 274-276.

THE CULTURALLY DEPRIVED

Barclay, D. L. Art education for the culturally different. *School Arts*, March 1970, pp. 14-17.

Barclay, D. L. (Ed.) *Art education for the disadvantaged child*. Washington: The National Art Education Association, 1969.

THE DEAF

Alkema, C. J. The exceptional child: The deaf. *School Arts*, November 1968, pp. 26, 27.

Bilger, G. Art helps the deaf develop language. *School Arts*, May 1961, pp. 13-15.

Conant, H., & Randall, A. W. The deaf. In *Art in education*. Peoria, Illinois: Charles A. Bennett, 1959, pp. 176, 177.

Cruickshank, W. M., & Johnson, G. O. The deaf. In *Education of exceptional children and youth*. Englewood Cliffs, New Jersey: Prentice Hall, 1958, p. 264.

James, C. G. Art and the adolescent deaf girl. *School Arts*, March 1955, pp. 21-22.

Jenson, P. M. Art helps the deaf to speak. *School Arts*, May 1959, pp. 9-10.

Kutis, H. S. Art, a voice in a world of silence. *Arts and Activities*, March 1966, pp. 18-20.

Lark-Horovitz, B., Lewis, H., & Luca, M. The deaf child. In *Understanding children's art for better teaching*. Columbus, Ohio: Charles E. Merrill, 1967, p. 143.

Lowenfeld, V. The deaf. In *Creative and mental growth*. New York: Macmillan, 1957 (3rd. ed.), pp. 474-477.

Lowenfeld, V. The deaf-blind. In *Creative and mental growth*. New York: Macmillan, 1957 (3rd. ed.), pp. 469-474.

Lowenfeld, V. The meaning of creative activity for the deaf-blind. *The Teachers Forum, American Foundation for the Blind*, 1940, Vol. XII.

Pintner, R. *Artistic appreciation among deaf children*. New York: American Association for the Deaf, 1941.

Schaettle, M. Art education for the deaf child. In *Art education for the exceptional child. Research Bulletin: Eastern Arts Association*. Kutztown, Pennsylvania: State Teachers College, 1956, pp. 26, 27.

Schilling, B. Another key: Art. *Volta Review*, October 1953, pp. 437, 438, 464.

THE EMOTIONALLY DISTURBED, THE MENTALLY ILL

Alschuler, R. H., & Hattwick, L. B. W. *Painting and personality: A study of young children*. Chicago, Illinois: University of Chicago Press, 1969.

Arlow, J. A., & Kadis, A. L. Finger painting in the psychotherapy of children. *American Journal of Orthopsychiatry*, 1946, *16*, 134-146.

Berkowitz, P. H., & Rothman, E. P. The creative arts. In *The disturbed child*. New York: New York University Press, 1960, pp. 160-175.

Berrien, F. K. A study of the drawings of abnormal children. *Journal of Educational Psychology*, 1935, *26*, pp. 143-150.

Bettelheim, B. Schizophrenic art: A case study. *Scientific American*, 1952, pp. 186-187.

Bhatt, M. Art and the socially maladjusted. *School Arts*, March 1955, pp. 23-25.

Conant, H., & Randall, A. W. Socially maladjusted. In *Art in education*. Peoria, Illinois: Charles A. Bennett, 1959, p. 179.

Cruickshank, W. M., & Johnson, G. O. The maladjusted and disturbed. In *Education of exceptional children and youth*. Englewood Cliffs, New Jersey: Prentice Hall, 1958, p. 592.

Davidson, B. E. Art meets the needs of behavior problem students. *Arts and Activities*, May 1966, pp. 24-26.

Eisner, E. Initiating art experiences for delinquent students. *Art Education*, February 1960, pp. 8, 9.

Freeman, R. V., & Friedman, I. Art therapy in mental illness. *School Arts*, March 1955, pp. 17-20.

Friedman, I. Art and therapy. *Psychoanalytic Review*, 1951, pp. 354-361.

Garton, M. Emotional release through creative painting for the mentally retarded. *American Childhood*, April 1952, pp. 10-12.

Gordon, J. Art helps free a troubled mind. *School Arts*, May 1959, pp. 13-14.

Harms, E. The arts as applied to psychotherapy. *Design*, 1945, Vol. 46, No. 6.

Henkes, R. Art and the professional guidance counselor. *School Arts*, May 1961, pp. 7-8.

Kellogg, R., & O'Dell, S. *The psychology of children's art*. New York: CRM-Random House, 1967.

Kramer, E. Art therapy at Wiltwyck School. *School Arts*, May 1959, pp. 5-8.

Kramer, E. *Art therapy in a children's community*. Springfield, Illinois: Charles C Thomas, 1958.

Kramer, E., & Helmuth, J. Art and the troubled child . . . A joint exhibition. *Art Education*, April 1960, pp. 6-9.

Kris, E. Psychoanalytic explorations in art. *The Psychoanalytic Quarterly*, 1953, Vol. XXII.

Lowenfeld, V. Self-adjustment through creative activity. *American Journal of Mental Deficiency*, 1941, Vol. XLV.

Lowenfeld, V. Therapeutic aspects of art education. In *Art education for the exceptional child. Research Bulletin: Eastern Arts Association*. Kutztown, Pennsylvania: State Teachers College, 1956, pp. 14-17.

Lowenfeld, V. The mentally retarded. In *Creative and mental growth*. New York: Macmillan, 1957 (3rd. ed.), pp. 484-494.

Mosse, E. P. Painting analysis in the therapy of neuroses. *Psycho-Analytical Review*, 1940.

Naumberg, M. *Schizophrenic art: Its meaning in psychotherapy*. New York: Grune and Stratton, 1959.

Naumberg, M. *Studies of the free art expression of behavior problem children*. New York: Grune and Company, 1947.

Naumberg, M. Studies of the "free" art expression of behavior problem children and adolescents as a means of diagnosis and therapy. *Nervous and Mental Disease Monographs*, 1947, No. 71.

Schaefer-Simmern, H., & Sarason, S. B. Therapeutic implications of artistic activity. *American Journal of Mental Deficiency*, 1944, Vol. 49.

Schaefer-Simmern, H. The experiment with delinquents. In *The unfolding of artistic activity*. Berkeley: University of California Press, 1940, pp. 68-95, 191-194.

THE GIFTED

Alkema, C. J. Art and the exceptional child: Part I: Implications of art for the gifted and the mentally retarded child. *Children's House*, Fall 1968, pp. 6-10. Part II: Implications of art for the gifted and the mentally retarded child. *Children's House*, Holiday issue 1968, pp. 12-15.

Art education in the secondary school. In *Bulletin of the National Association of Secondary School Principals*, March 1961, pp. 23-24.

Bauer, C., & Mead, R. A. Gifted children and art. *American Childhood*, September 1957, pp. 4-7.

Cane, F. The gifted child in art. *Journal of Educational Sociology*, October 1936, pp. 67-73.

Carter, T. M., & Geyer, P. A report on gifted children's reactions to arts and crafts stimuli. *Arts and Activities*, May 1959, pp. 28, 29, 42.

Conant, H., & Randall, A. W. The gifted. In *Art in education*. Peoria, Illinois: Charles A. Bennett, 1959, pp. 179-185.

de Francesco, I. Art and the exceptional child, *and* The gifted. In *Art education: Its means and ends*. New York: Harper, 1958, pp. 384-413 and 399-413.

Gaitskell, C. D. Art for gifted pupils. *School Arts*, March 1955, pp. 9-12.

Gaitskell, C. D., & Hurwitz, A. Art activities for gifted children. In *Children and their art*. New York: Harcourt, Brace and World, 1970, pp. 353-375.

Goldman, R. D. Art education for the gifted child. In *Art education for the exceptional child. Research Bulletin: Eastern Arts Association*. Kutztown, Pennsylvania: State Teachers College, 1956, pp. 17-20.

Lark-Horovitz, B., Lewis, H., & Luca, M. The artistically talented child. In *Understanding children's art for better teaching*. Columbus, Ohio: Charles E. Merrill, 1967, pp. 121-141.

Lowenfeld, V. The case of the gifted child. *School Arts*, April 1966, pp. 13-18.

Lowenfeld, V. The case of the gifted child. In *Creative and mental growth*. New York: Macmillan, 1957 (3rd. ed.), pp. 420-429.

Lowenfeld, V. The gifted child. In *Creative and mental growth*. New York: Macmillan, 1964 (4th. ed.), pp. 381-394.

McFee, J. K. Creative problem solving abilities in art of academically superior adolescents [an experimental study of problem solving approaches to design and creative behavior]. Washington: The National Art Education Association, 1968.

Tumin, M. M. The gifted child in a democratic society. In *Art education for the exceptional child. Research Bulletin: Eastern Arts Association*. Kutztown, Pennsylvania: State Teachers College, 1956, pp. 8-10.

Wasserman, B. The exceptionally gifted in art. *School Arts*, May 1959, pp. 19-20.

THE MENTALLY RETARDED

Achrach, B. Retarded children meet the masters. *Arts and Activities*, June 1960, pp. 20, 21, 37.

Alkema, C. J. Art and the exceptional child. Part I: Implications of art for the gifted and the mentally retarded child. *Children's House*, Fall 1968, pp. 6-10. Part II: Implications of art for the gifted and the mentally retarded child. *Children's House*, Holiday issue 1968, pp. 12-15.

Art education in the secondary school. In *Bulletin of the National Association of Secondary School Principals*, March 1961, pp. 21-22.

Baskin, J. W. Retarded children need art. *School Arts*, March 1955, pp. 13-15.

Conant, H., & Randall, A. W. Mentally retarded. In *Art in education*. Peoria, Illinois: Charles A. Bennett, 1959, pp. 177-178.

Cruickshank, W. M., & Johnson, G. O. The mentally deficient. In *Education of exceptional children in youth*. Englewood Cliffs, New Jersey: Prentice Hall, 1958, p. 253.

de Francesco, I. The mentally retarded. In *Art education: Its means and ends*. New York: Harper, 1958, pp. 395-397.

Emlen, M. G. Art and the slow learner. *School Arts*, March 1970, pp. 10-12.

Gaitskell, C. D. *Art education for slow learners*. Peoria, Illinois: Charles A. Bennett, 1953.

Gaitskell, C. D. Art education for slow learners. *School Arts*, February 1954, pp. 9-12.

Gaitskell, C. D., & Hurwitz, A. Art activities for slow learners. In *Children and their art*. New York: Harcourt, Brace and World, 1970, pp. 324-352.

Garton, M. Emotional release through creative painting for the mentally retarded. *American Childhood*, April 1952, pp. 10-12.

Goslin, J. Students bring art to retarded adults. *School Arts*, May 1959, pp. 17-18.

Kirk, S. A., & Johnson, G. O. *Educating the retarded child*. Cambridge, Massachusetts: Riverside Press, 1951, pp. 300-309.

Lane, J. C. Art education for the mentally retarded child. In *Art education for the exceptional child. Research Bulletin: Eastern Arts Association.* Kutztown, Pennsylvania: State Teachers College, 1956, pp. 26-27.

Lark-Horovitz, B., Lewis, H., & Luca, M. The retarded child. In *Understanding children's art for better teaching.* Columbus, Ohio: Charles E. Merrill, 1967, pp. 141-143.

Lowenfeld, V. The mentally retarded. In *Creative and mental growth.* New York: MacMillan, 1957 (3rd. ed.), pp. 484-494.

McMillin, B. Stitchery and the retarded child. *School Arts*, January 1964, pp. 18-19.

McNiece, W., & Benson, K. R. *Crafts for the retarded.* Bloomington, Illinois: McKnight and McKnight, 1964.

Pollock, M. P., & Pollock, M. New hope for the retarded. Boston: Porter Sargent, 1953, pp. 89-90.

Rapaport, I. The art of the mentally retarded child. *School Arts*, January 1964, pp. 13-17.

Rothstein. The arts. In *Mental retardation.* New York: Holt, Rinehart, Winston, 1961, pp. 260-269.

Schaffer-Simmern, H. The experiment with·mental defectives. In *The unfolding of artistic activity.* Berkeley: University of California Press, 1940, pp. 36-69; also pp. 183-191.

Semmel, M. I. Art education for the mentally retarded. *School Arts*, May 1961, pp. 17-20.

Sisk, P. A. A sequential program to develop textural sensitivity. *School Arts*, January 1964, pp. 21-26.

Sisters of St. Francis of Assisi, St. Coletta Schools. *Art education curriculum for the mentally retarded.* Milwaukee, Wisconsin: Department of Special Education, The Cardinal Stritch College, 1959.

Sisters of St. Francis of Assisi, St. Coletta Schools. *Crafts curriculum for the mentally handicapped.* Milwaukee, Wisconsin: Department of Special Education, The Cardinal Stritch College, 1960.

Stein, M. Art as a means of expression for the mentally retarded. *Exceptional Children*, March 1938, p. 141.

Steinhauser, M. N. Art for the mentally retarded child. *School Arts*, March 1970, pp. 30-31.

Vandervoort, P. Art of the mentally retarded on exhibition. *School Arts*, January 1964, pp. 10-12.

Von Bargen, D. Motivating an art experience. *The Instructor*, September 1965, pp. 142-143.

THE PHYSICALLY HANDICAPPED

Alkema, C. J. Implications for art for the handicapped child. *Exceptional Children*, February 1967, pp. 433, 434.

Conant, H., & Randall, A. W. Physically handicapped. In *Art in education.* Peoria, Illinois: Charles A. Bennett, 1959, pp. 178-179.

Cruickshank, W. M., & Johnson, G. O. The crippled. In *Education of exceptional children and youth.* Englewood Cliffs, New Jersey: Prentice Hall, 1958, pp. 466, 467, 474.

Cyr, D. Everybody makes the scene. *Arts and Activities*, April 1970, pp. 26-28.

Fouracre, M. H. The handicapped child in a democratic society. In *Art education for the exceptional child. Research Bulletin: Eastern Arts Association.* Kutztown, Pennsylvania: State Teachers College, 1956, pp. 11-13.

Lowenfeld, V. The cerebral palsied, *and* The crippled. In *Creative and mental growth.* New York: MacMillan, 1957 (3rd ed.), pp. 478-481 *and* 481-484.

Marksberry, M. L. Creative experiences in recreational activities for crippled children. *Exceptional Children*, September 1958, pp. 90-91.

Nagy, G. Cerebral palsied discover art. *School Arts*, May 1959, pp. 15-16.

Parker, J. A. Art and the special child. *School Arts*, March 1970, pp. 32-33.

Scheerer, D. T. Art and the cerebral palsied. *School Arts*, December 1962, pp. 15-17.

THE SPEECH DEFECTIVE

Conant, H., & Randall, A. W. Speech defects. In *Art in education.* Peoria, Illinois: Charles A. Bennett, 1959, p. 177.

Lowenfeld, V. The stutterer, *and* The speech defective. In *Creative and mental growth.* New York: MacMillan, 1957 (3rd. ed.), pp. 477-478.

THE VISUALLY HANDICAPPED

Anderson, M. Art for the visually handicapped. *School Arts*, June 1956, pp. 21-23.

Andrews. Art experiences for blind children. *The International Journal of Instructors of the Blind*, May 1956.

Bains, M. Art and blind children. *School Arts*, January 1964, pp. 3-9.

Borodziej, I. The visually handicapped youngster in art. *School Arts*, January 1964, pp. 27-28.

Buell, C. E. Hobbies and other leisure time activities. In *Recreation for the blind.* New York: American Foundation for the Blind, pp. 14-17.

Burgart, H. J. Art helps teach sight by touch. *School Arts*, May 1959, pp. 11-12.

Combs, P. He gives the blind the gift of inner vision. *Reader's Digest*, August 1961, pp. 207-212.

Conant, H., & Randall, A. W. The blind, *and* The partially seeing. In *Art in education*. Peoria, Illinois: Charles A. Bennett, 1959, pp. 174-175 *and* 175-176.

Conant, H. Experiencing creativity after blindness. *School Arts*, May 1961, pp. 23-24.

Cutsforth, T. D. The esthetic life of the blind. In *The blind in school and society*. New York: American Foundation for the Blind, pp. 166-194.

Decker. Creative art experiences for blind children. *The International Journal of Instructors of the Blind*, May 1960, p. 104.

de Francesco, I. The blind. In *Art education: Its means and ends*. New York: Harper, 1958, pp. 392-395.

Eaton, A. H. *Beauty for the sighted and blind*. New York: St. Martin's Press, 1959 [an excellent book on art appreciation for the blind].

Haupt, C. Clay modeling—A means and an end. In G. L. Abel (Comp.), *Concerning the education of blind children*. New York: American Foundation for the Blind, 1959, pp. 65-68.

Heyman, C. Art for the blind. *School Arts*, March 1955, p. 16.

Jones, C. R. Art for the blind and partially seeing. *School Arts*, May 1961, pp. 21-22.

Kerwell, J. *Sculpture by blind children*. New York: American Foundation for the Blind, 1955.

Kurzhals. Creating with material can be of value for young blind children. *The International Journal of Instructors of the Blind*, March 1961, p. 75.

Lark-Horovitz, B., Lewis, H., & Luca, M. The blind child. In *Understanding children's art for better teaching*. Columbus, Ohio: Charles E. Merrill, 1967, pp. 143-144.

Lodholz. Ceramics for the blind. *Journal of the American Association of Instructors of the Blind*, 1950, p. 197.

Lowenfeld, V. The blind. In *Creative and mental growth*. New York: Macmillan, 1957 (3rd. ed.), pp. 443-469.

Lowenfeld, V. The meaning of creative activity for the deaf-blind. *The Teachers Forum, American Foundation for the Blind*, 1940, *Vol. XII*.

Lowenfeld, V. Modeling as a means of self-expression in the schools for the blind. *The Harvard Educational Review*, 1942, *Vol. XII, No. 1*.

Mattsson. Silver: A creative medium for the blind craftsman. *Journal of the American Association of Instructors of the Blind*, 1950, p. 189.

Revesz, G. *Psychology and the art of the blind*. New York: Longmans, Green, 1950.

Roderick, R. . . . A matter of feeling. . . . *Arts and Activities*, January 1964, pp. 26, 27.

Roderick, R. Exceptional children develop through art expression. *The International Journal of Instructors of the Blind*, April 1956.

TECHNIQUES

The books and articles listed are all by Professor Alkema; in many instances, they describe techniques suitable for use by exceptional children.

Portraits in depth. *Arts and Activities*, October 1963, pp. 33, 34.

The want ads reclassified. *Arts and Activities*, December 1963, pp. 21, 22.

Paper mache animals. *School Arts*, March 1964, pp. 16, 17.

Weaving in the elementary grades. *Arts and Activities*, March 1964, pp. 22-24.

Weaving in the elementary grades: Part II. *Arts and Activities*, April 1964, Cover and pp. 20-23.

Creative copper tooling. *Arts and Activities*, June 1964, pp. 6, 7.

Non-scientific insect mobiles. *School Arts*, November 1964, pp. 10-13.

Window transparencies: Part I. Tissue hits the holiday spot. *Arts and Activities*, November 1964, pp. 13-15.

Window transparencies: Part II. Flaming windows set Christmas mood. . . . *Arts and Activities*, December 1964, pp. 16-18.

This is a puppet any child can make. *Grade Teacher*, February 1965, pp. 68, 93.

Magnificent mosaics. . . . *Arts and Activities*, February 1965, pp. 26-29.

Graph paper designs. *Grade Teacher*, April 1965, pp. 44, 45.

Kids create their own "pop" art. *Arts and Activities*, May 1965, pp. 11-13.

Paper mache. *The Instructor*, September 1965, pp. 85, 86.

Masks in art and history: Part I: The development of masks from prehistoric to modern times. *Arts and Activities*, September 1965, pp. 18-22.

Masks in art and history: Part II: Appropriate methods, materials and techniques for mask-making. *Arts and Activities*, October 1965, cover and pp. 8-12.

Three-dimensional possibilities of paper. *The Instructor*, May 1966, pp. 79-86. Reprinted in *Saber*, March through August 1967.

The Gothic Age revived. *Design*, May-June 1966, pp. 22-25.

The art of making puppets. *Design*, September-October 1966, pp. 29-33.

Things to make. *Grade Teacher*, November 1966, p. 92.

Printing . . . An art you can put to use. *The Instructor*, December 1966, p. 30.

Christmas Eve on our street. *School Arts*, December 1966, pp. 12, 13.

Creative paper crafts in color. New York: Sterling Publishing Company, 1967.

Crayon and chalk stencil technique. *School Arts*, March 1967, pp. 38-41.

We rode a space capsule. *The Instructor*, April 1967, p. 134.

Let's progress beyond the lollipop tree. *Design*, Summer 1967, pp. 4-8.

Tooling aluminum. *Design*, Summer 1967, pp. 28-29.

Birds from another planet. *Grade Teacher*, September 1967, pp. 120-121.

Paper weaving. *The Instructor*, October 1967, pp. 142-143.

Studying detail through figure collage. . . . *Arts and Activities*, February 1968, pp. 24, 25.

Depicting the human figure in art. *Design*, Mid-winter issue 1968, pp. 14-19.

Learning to see on a looking walk. *Arts and Activities*, June 1968, pp. 32-35.

This is what I saw on my vacation. *Arts and Activities*, September 1968, pp. 30-32.

The crayon: Part I. *The Instructor*, October 1968, pp. 108-111. Part II. *The Instructor*, November 1968, pp. 72-75. Reprinted in *Saber*, May through July and September through November 1969.

I wonder as I wander. *Arts and Activities*, November 1968, pp. 20-22.

Exploring with the crayon etching technique: Part I. *Design*, Fall 1968, pp. 6-12.

Exploring with the crayon etching technique: Part II. *Design*, Winter 1968, pp. 6-11.

Simulated stained window etching. *Design*, Winter 1968, pp. 20-23.

The complete crayon book in color. New York: Sterling Publishing Company, 1969.

Scrap materials: A source of motivation in art. *Design*, Fall 1969, pp. 4-9.

Experimenting with tempera. *Design*, Mid-winter 1970, cover and pp. 26-30.

Fabricate tu propia mascara (Create your own masks). In *Fantasta Juvenil*. New York: A Spanish Language Readers Digest Condensed Book for Children, pp. 126-129.

Exploring with melted wax crayon. *Design*, Summer 1970, pp. 4-7.

Index